DRUMSET COORDINA

A METHOD FOR DEVELOPING COMPLETE INDEPEND

BY BLAKE PAULSON

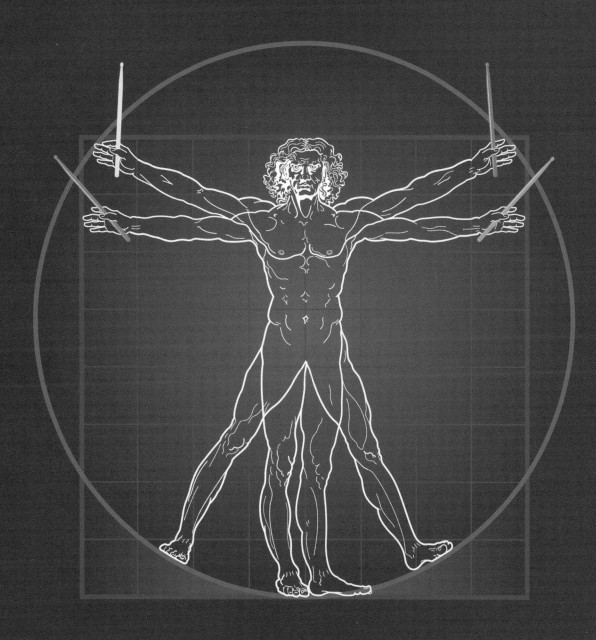

ISBN 978-1-4768-1333-2

HAL•LEONARD®
CORPORATION

7777 W. BLUEMOUND RD. P.O. BOX 13819 MILWAUKEE, WI 53213

In Australia Contact:
Hal Leonard Australia Pty. Ltd.
4 Lentara Court
Cheltenham, Victoria, 3192 Australia
Email: ausadmin@halleonard.com.au

Visit Hal Leonard Online at
www.halleonard.com

INTRODUCTION

Welcome to *Drumset Coordination*, a comprehensive practice tool designed to help you gain coordination, independence, control, creativity, and musicality on the drumset. The goal of this book is to help you obtain these skills in an efficient and well-organized manner. I hope you enjoy this book and have fun improving and growing as a musician.

ACKNOWLEDGMENTS

Photo courtesy of Sue Bowen
www.suebowen.com

This book is dedicated to Bridget Kleinberg. You have helped me in more ways than I can express. Thank you. Turtle.

My deepest thanks to my family for guiding, supporting, and enlightening me: John Paulson; Coreen Nordling; Emily Paulson; Kevin Donnelly; Steve, Denise, Spencer, and Patrick Cronin; Patti, Kent, and Reina Hardy; Ray, Susan, Duke, and Andrea Paulson; and all of my extended family.

Thanks to my teachers for their inspiration: Scott Crosbie, Paul Stueber, Dave DiCenso, Stan Freese, and Brian and Jane Grivna.

Thanks to Jeff Schroedl and Jackie Muth at Hal Leonard, Bryan Scheidecker at Vic Firth, Andrew Meskin at Drum Workshop, and Juan Zavala at Guitar Center Pro.

Thanks to my students for helping me test and improve this book from first draft to the current edition. You rock!

Lastly, I would like to thank the talented singers, songwriters, producers, and musicians I work with. You motivate me to practice and create more every day.

HOW TO USE THIS BOOK

Drumset Coordination is designed for all drummers. To use this book you will need an understanding of how to play the drumset and read drumset notation. You can play each lesson in order or work on individual lessons to strengthen specific aspects of coordination. For advanced and professional drummers, this material can be studied on your own. For beginning and intermediate drummers, this book should be studied with the help of a private teacher who can demonstrate the lessons and explain how they can be applied in musical situations.

Each lesson consists of six steps that create true 4-way independence on the drumset.

- **Step 1:** This is an ostinato (repeating pattern) that you play continuously with one of your feet throughout the lesson.
- **Step 2:** These are ostinatos that you play continuously with your remaining foot throughout the lesson. You will play each rhythm presented as an individual lesson with the other five steps.
- **Step 3:** This is an ostinato that you play continuously with one of your hands throughout the lesson.
- **Steps 4 and 5:** With your remaining free hand, play each rhythm presented in these steps as a separate exercise, repeating each until mastered.
- **Step 6:** With your remaining free hand, play this summary exercise, repeating until mastered.

To get started, turn on your metronome and build each lesson by adding one step at a time. Step 2 provides many bass drum rhythms to practice; choose one. I suggest a tempo between 60–140 beats per minute. Focus on rhythmic accuracy and a smooth performance until you are comfortable with the new coordination. Do not focus on playing overly fast as this will not help your muscles memorize the new skills.

Play each rhythm in Steps 4 and 5 as its own exercise. There is no correct number of times to play each of these rhythms; play them until you achieve a smooth, consistent, and confident performance before moving on to the next rhythm. If you get stuck, try these ideas:

- Decrease your tempo.
- Play Steps 1, 2, 3 and count Step 4 or 5 out loud until it is internalized, then play it.
- Play only Steps 3 and 4 or 3 and 5 until comfortable, then add Steps 1 and 2 back in.
- Consult your private teacher.

When you complete the six steps, check off the bass drum rhythm you played and write down your practice tempo. Choose a new bass drum rhythm to practice and repeat the six steps. Continue this until you have practiced every bass drum rhythm with every step in the lesson. It's normal to spend many practice hours on each lesson. Therefore, do not rush to complete the book. Focus on the execution of what you are learning.

NOTES FOR SECTIONS ONE AND TWO: When playing Steps 5 and 6 you may notice increased difficulty reading triplet rhythms against eighths or sixteenths. To help you visualize how these rhythms fit together, I have included a notation guide on page v. If Steps 5 and 6 feel too advanced for you, play through these lessons reading Step 4 only. You can return to play Steps 5 and 6 when you're ready.

NOTES FOR SECTION THREE: Step 5 provides a variety of fundamental Afro-Cuban and Latin rhythms. Make note of the clave direction: 3–2 or 2–3. Typically you will want to align Steps 2, 3, and 5 to have the same clave direction. However, you may also want to experiment with the clave working in opposite directions. For more information on clave, please consult your private teacher.

These lessons are a fun and rewarding challenge. When done properly, they will greatly improve your drumming.

BALANCE

This book is a powerful practice tool, but it represents only one aspect of being a well-rounded drummer. I suggest using this book as part of a balanced practice routine. Also, if at any time your hands or feet become sore or tired from playing these lessons, stop and take a break! Injury from overuse is to be avoided.

CONCENTRATION

The ability to concentrate and maintain focus while performing music is crucial. Without a high degree of concentration, parts are more likely to be executed with mistakes and inaccuracies. During a performance there can be many kinds of distractions. Upon completion of this book, you will find that you have a much deeper sense of focus. These lessons require you to execute challenging 4-way coordination while reading music. In addition, you must listen to yourself and analyze your performance for accuracy. Exercising your mind in this way will sharpen your ability to concentrate.

CONFIDENCE

This book provides you with a vast amount of coordination challenges. Once you have mastered these lessons, you will feel great confidence by having gained a remarkable amount of coordination and independence on the drumset. Your new skills will provide the ability to play very difficult and electrifying grooves. Moreover, you will have the tools to quickly learn new grooves; this is especially important when working with producers and music directors who may want you to play unexpected and unusual drum grooves on the fly. With your new confidence, you can tackle any curveballs head on.

CREATIVITY

The sky is the limit on your personal creativity. The more time you invest in practicing your drumset, the more creative your musical ideas will become. Mastering the lessons in this book will greatly enhance this. You will have the ability to mix and match numerous rhythms with each hand and foot, thereby giving you the freedom to play virtually anything your mind dreams up.

Be sure to consider orchestration. I encourage you to test your newly earned independence on as many different drums, cymbals, and percussion instruments as you can. That new groove you're about to create may be something the world has never heard before. Above all else, be creative and have fun!

NOTATION GUIDE

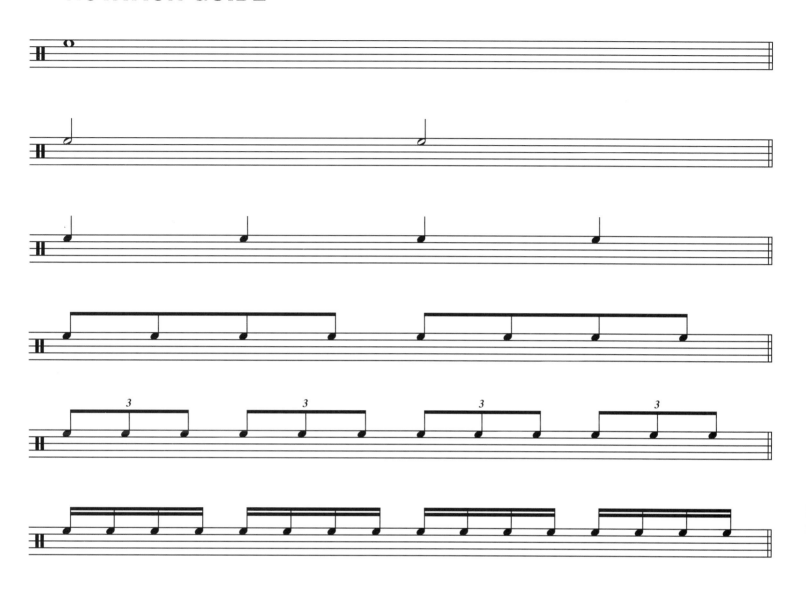

DRUM KEY

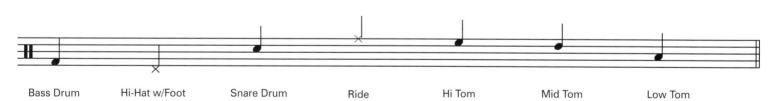

| Bass Drum | Hi-Hat w/Foot | Snare Drum | Ride | Hi Tom | Mid Tom | Low Tom |

CONTENTS

SECTION ONE
ROCK • POP • R&B • COUNTRY

LESSON 1.1

STEP 1 · Start by playing either of these ostinatos on the Hi-Hat Foot:

STEP 2 · Continue step 1 and add one of these ostinatos on the Bass Drum:

STEP 3 · Continue steps 1, 2 and add this ostinato on the Ride Cymbal:

STEP 4 · Continue steps 1, 2, 3 and add each of these rhythms on the Snare Drum:

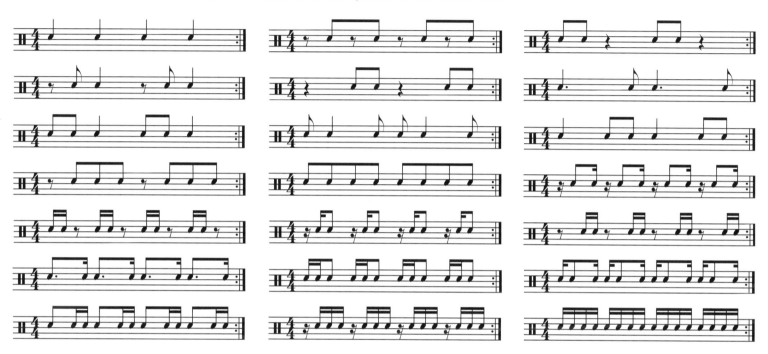

STEP 5 · Continue steps 1, 2, 3 and add each of these rhythms on the Snare Drum:

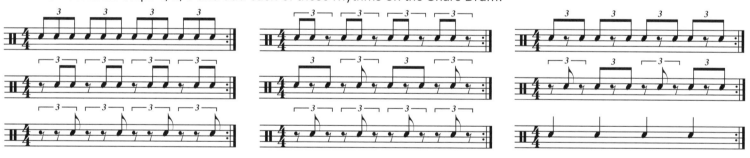

STEP 6 · Continue steps 1, 2, 3 and play this 8-bar exercise on the Snare Drum:

LESSON 1.2

STEP 1 · Start by playing either of these ostinatos on the Hi-Hat Foot:

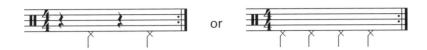

STEP 2 · Continue step 1 and add one of these ostinatos on the Bass Drum:

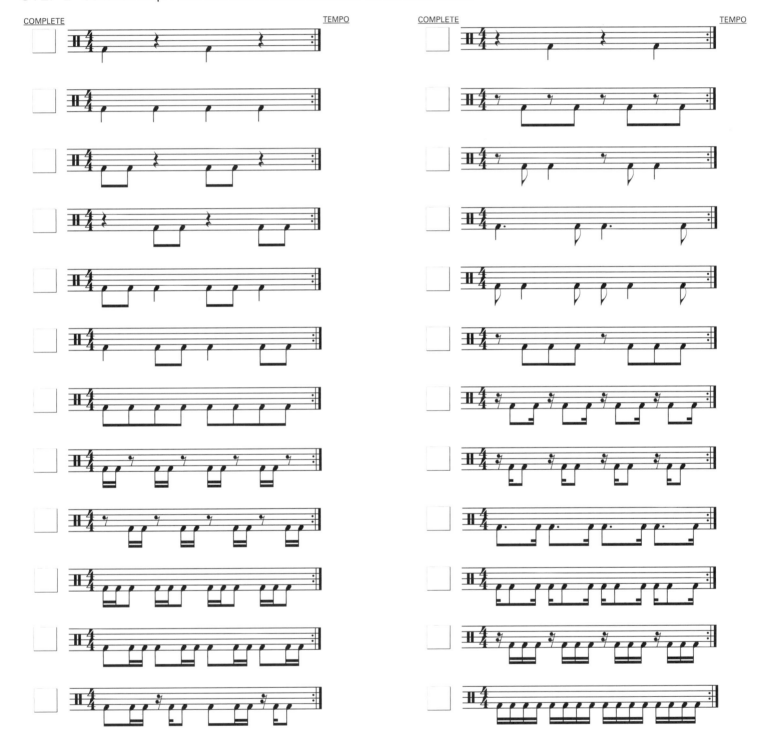

STEP 3 · Continue steps 1, 2 and add this ostinato on the Ride Cymbal:

STEP 4 · Continue steps 1, 2, 3 and add each of these rhythms on the Snare Drum:

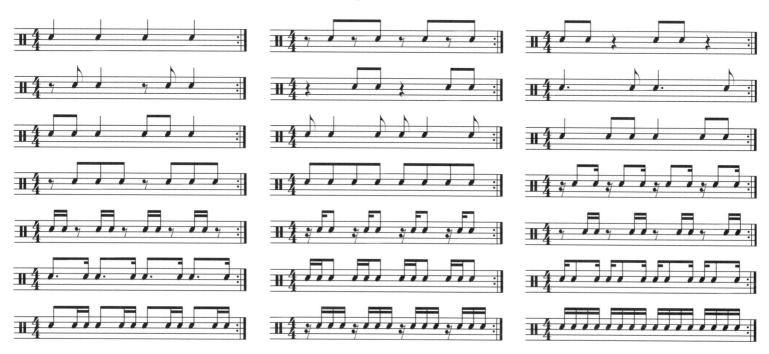

STEP 5 · Continue steps 1, 2, 3 and add each of these rhythms on the Snare Drum:

STEP 6 · Continue steps 1, 2, 3 and play this 8-bar exercise on the Snare Drum:

LESSON 1.3

STEP 1 · Start by playing either of these ostinatos on the Hi-Hat Foot:

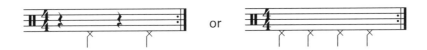

STEP 2 · Continue step 1 and add one of these ostinatos on the Bass Drum:

6

STEP 3 · Continue steps 1, 2 and add this ostinato on the Ride Cymbal:

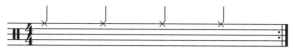

STEP 4 · Continue steps 1, 2, 3 and add each of these rhythms on the Snare Drum:

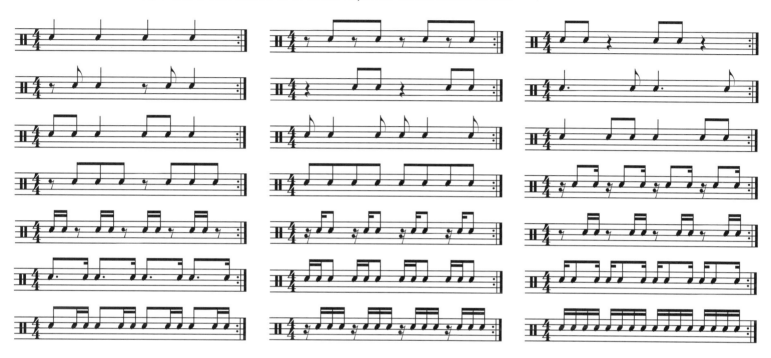

STEP 5 · Continue steps 1, 2, 3 and add each of these rhythms on the Snare Drum:

STEP 6 · Continue steps 1, 2, 3 and play this 8-bar exercise on the Snare Drum:

LESSON 1.4

STEP 1 · Start by playing either of these ostinatos on the Hi-Hat Foot:

STEP 2 · Continue step 1 and add one of these ostinatos on the Bass Drum:

STEP 3 · Continue steps 1, 2 and add this ostinato on the Ride Cymbal:

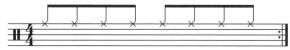

STEP 4 · Continue steps 1, 2, 3 and add each of these rhythms on the Snare Drum:

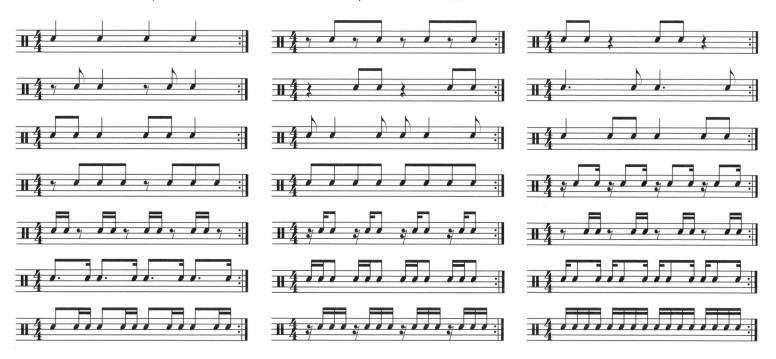

STEP 5 · Continue steps 1, 2, 3 and add each of these rhythms on the Snare Drum:

STEP 6 · Continue steps 1, 2, 3 and play this 8-bar exercise on the Snare Drum:

LESSON 1.5

STEP 1 · Start by playing either of these ostinatos on the Hi-Hat Foot:

STEP 2 · Continue step 1 and add one of these ostinatos on the Bass Drum:

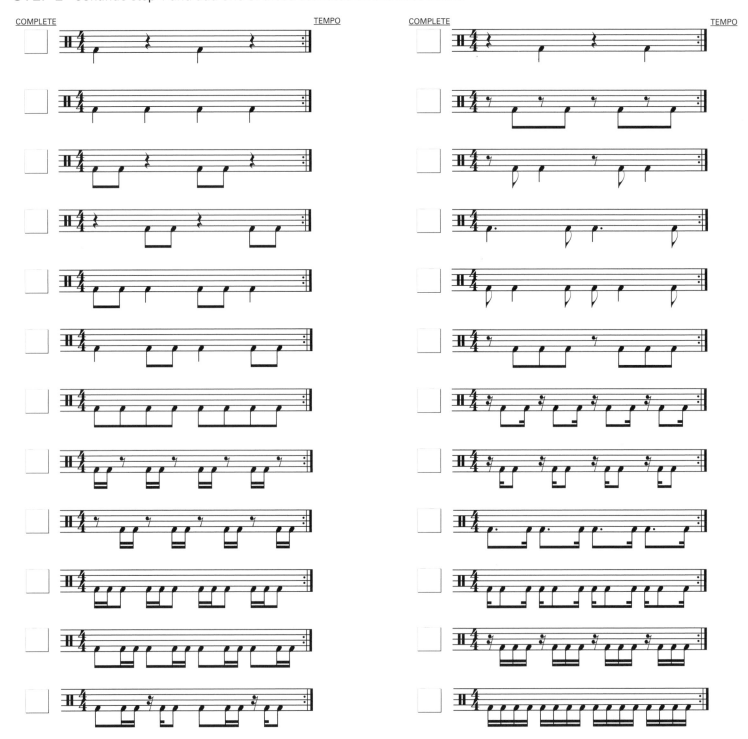

STEP 3 · Continue steps 1, 2 and add this ostinato on the Ride Cymbal:

STEP 4 · Continue steps 1, 2, 3 and add each of these rhythms on the Snare Drum:

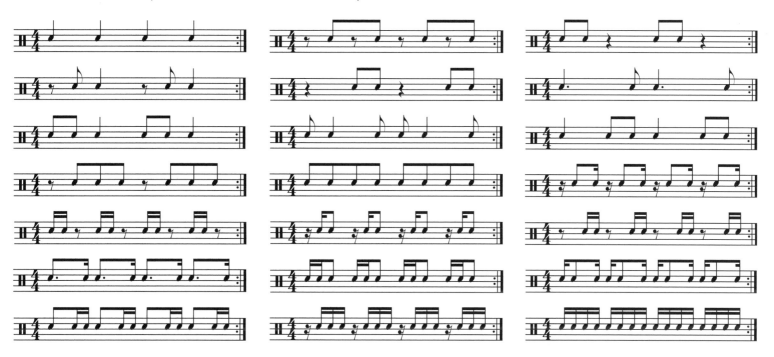

STEP 5 · Continue steps 1, 2, 3 and add each of these rhythms on the Snare Drum:

STEP 6 · Continue steps 1, 2, 3 and play this 8-bar exercise on the Snare Drum:

LESSON 1.6

STEP 1 · Start by playing either of these ostinatos on the Hi-Hat Foot:

STEP 2 · Continue step 1 and add one of these ostinatos on the Bass Drum:

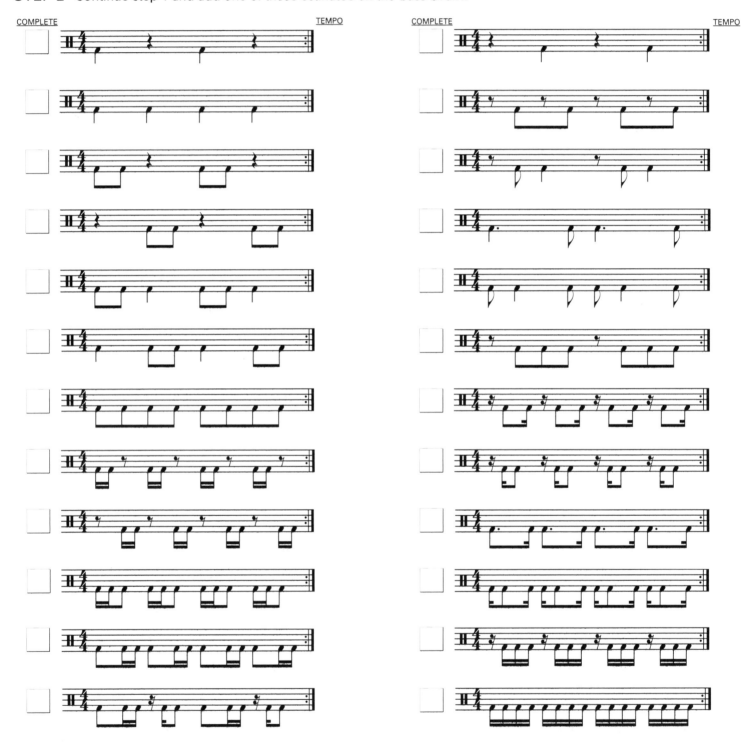

STEP 3 · Continue steps 1, 2 and add this ostinato on the Ride Cymbal:

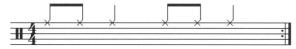

STEP 4 · Continue steps 1, 2, 3 and add each of these rhythms on the Snare Drum:

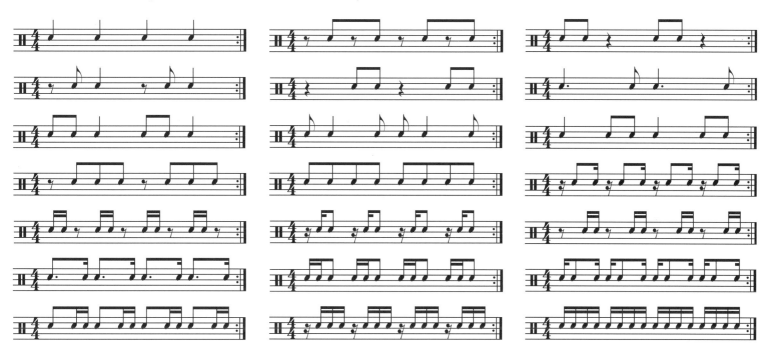

STEP 5 · Continue steps 1, 2, 3 and add each of these rhythms on the Snare Drum:

STEP 6 · Continue steps 1, 2, 3 and play this 8-bar exercise on the Snare Drum:

LESSON 1.7

STEP 1 · Start by playing either of these ostinatos on the Hi-Hat Foot:

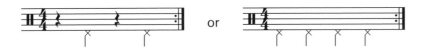

STEP 2 · Continue step 1 and add one of these ostinatos on the Bass Drum:

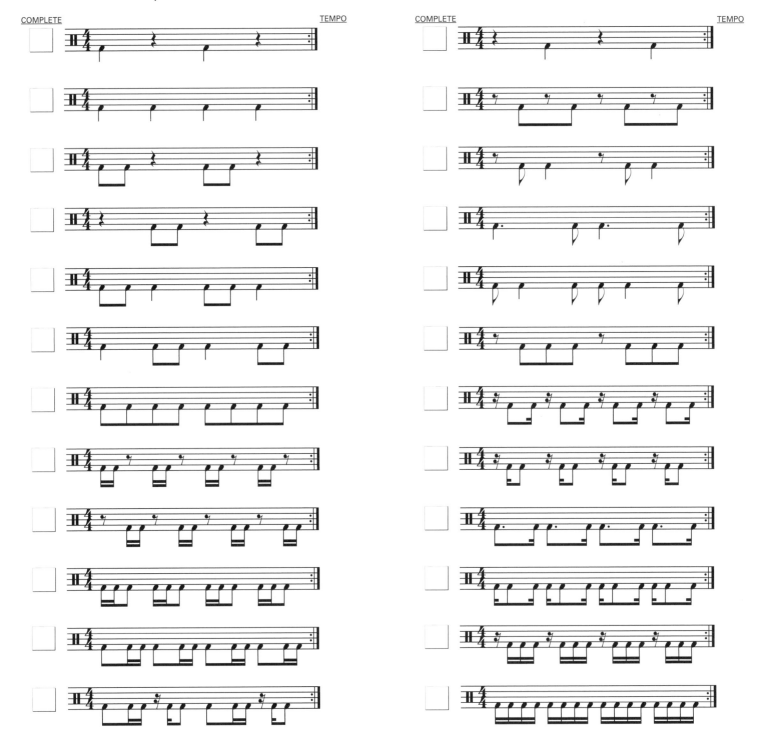

STEP 3 · Continue steps 1, 2 and add this ostinato on the Ride Cymbal:

STEP 4 · Continue steps 1, 2, 3 and add each of these rhythms on the Snare Drum:

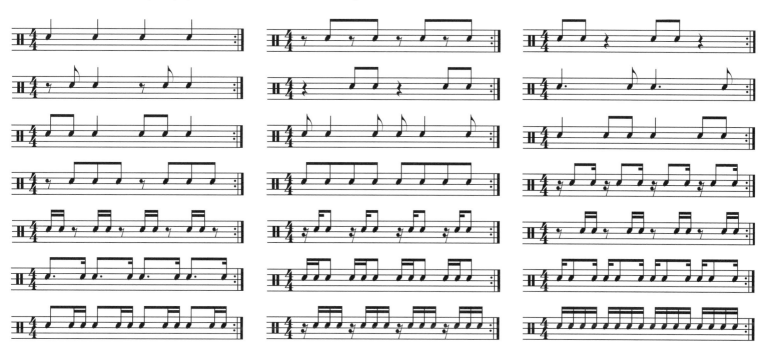

STEP 5 · Continue steps 1, 2, 3 and add each of these rhythms on the Snare Drum:

STEP 6 · Continue steps 1, 2, 3 and play this 8-bar exercise on the Snare Drum:

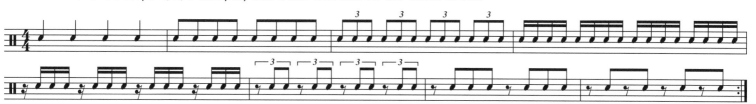

LESSON 1.8

STEP 1 · Start by playing either of these ostinatos on the Hi-Hat Foot:

or

STEP 2 · Continue step 1 and add one of these ostinatos on the Bass Drum:

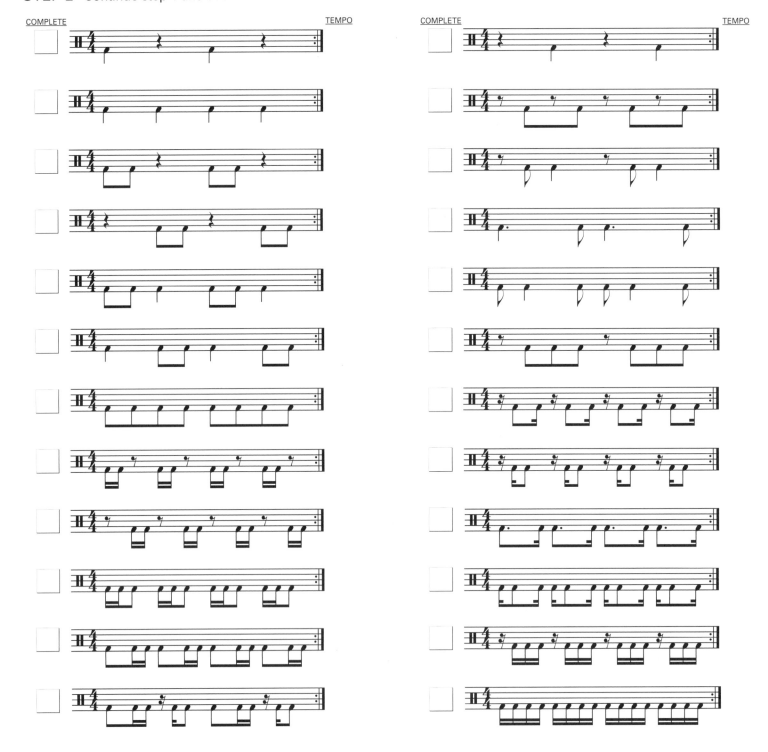

STEP 3 · Continue steps 1, 2 and add this ostinato on the Ride Cymbal:

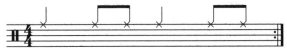

STEP 4 · Continue steps 1, 2, 3 and add each of these rhythms on the Snare Drum:

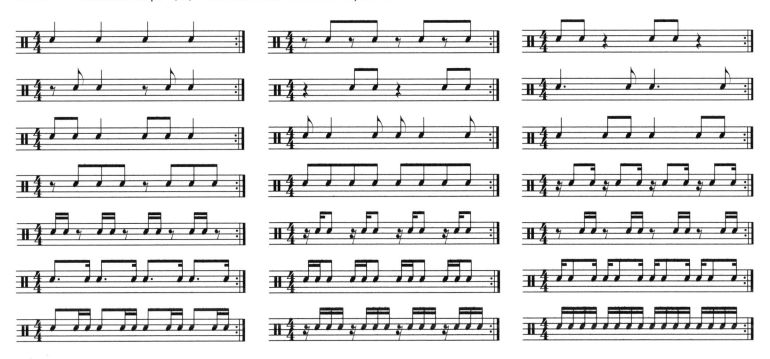

STEP 5 · Continue steps 1, 2, 3 and add each of these rhythms on the Snare Drum:

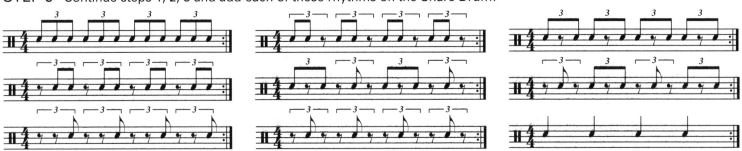

STEP 6 · Continue steps 1, 2, 3 and play this 8-bar exercise on the Snare Drum:

LESSON 1.9

STEP 1 · Start by playing either of these ostinatos on the Hi-Hat Foot:

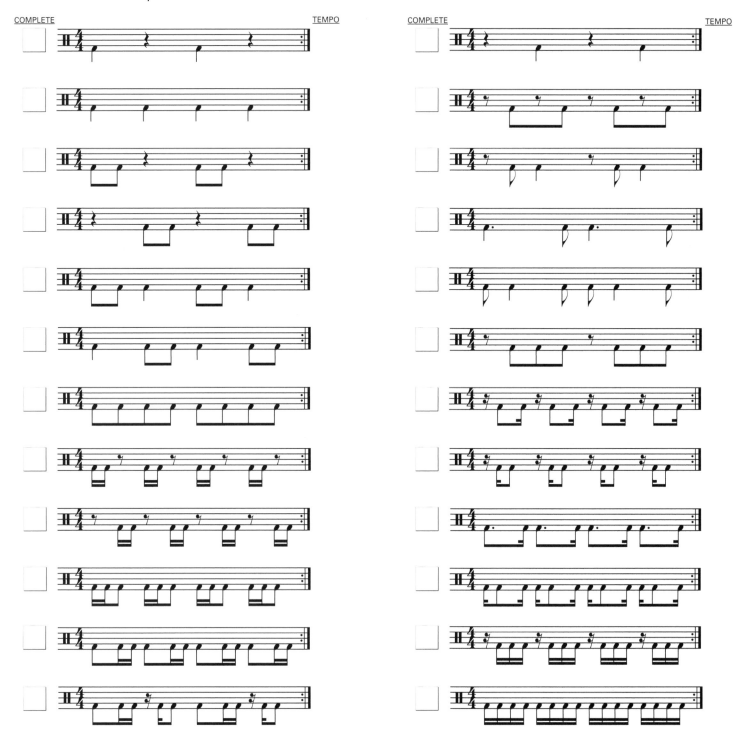

STEP 3 · Continue steps 1, 2 and add this ostinato on the Ride Cymbal:

STEP 4 · Continue steps 1, 2, 3 and add each of these rhythms on the Snare Drum:

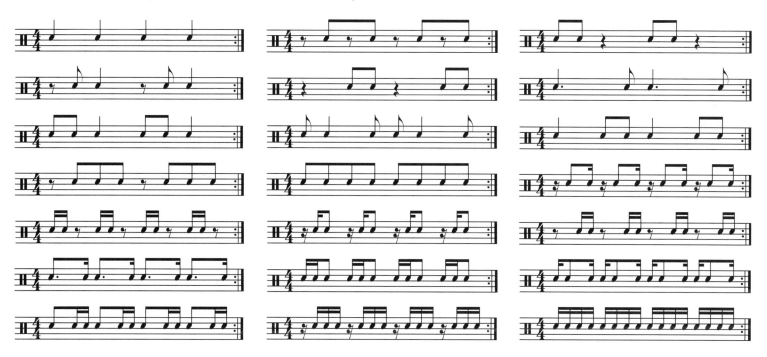

STEP 5 · Continue steps 1, 2, 3 and add each of these rhythms on the Snare Drum:

STEP 6 · Continue steps 1, 2, 3 and play this 8-bar exercise on the Snare Drum:

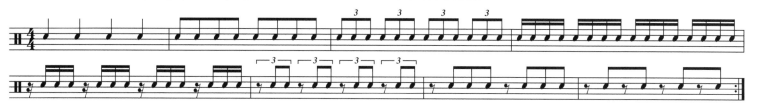

LESSON 1.10

STEP 1 · Start by playing either of these ostinatos on the Hi-Hat Foot:

STEP 2 · Continue step 1 and add one of these ostinatos on the Bass Drum:

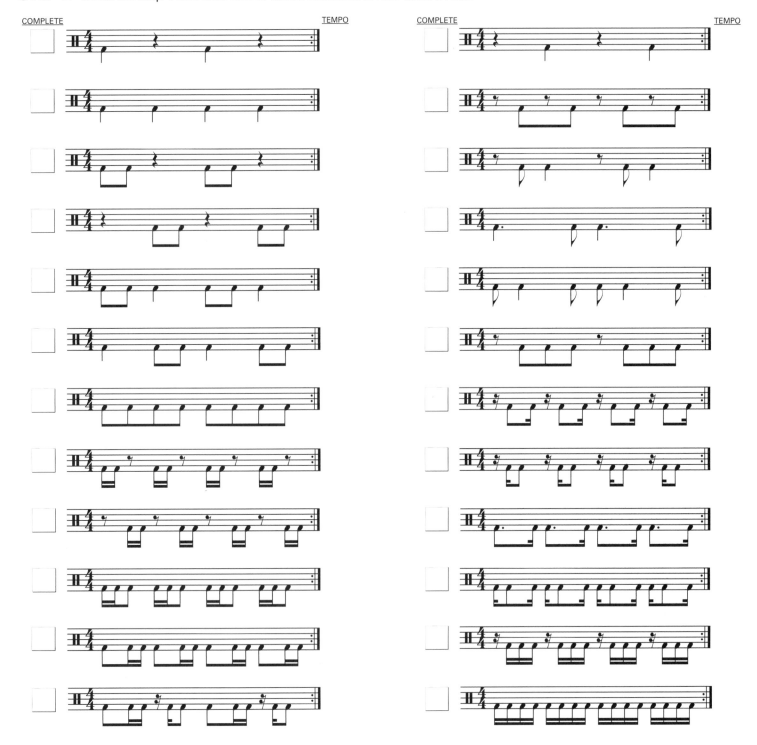

STEP 3 · Continue steps 1, 2 and add this ostinato on the Ride Cymbal:

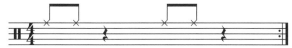

STEP 4 · Continue steps 1, 2, 3 and add each of these rhythms on the Snare Drum:

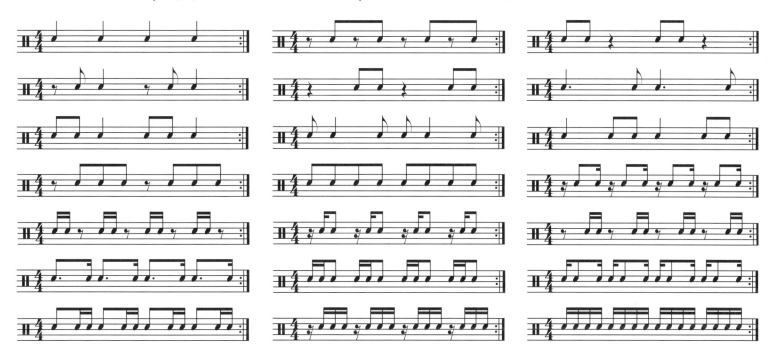

STEP 5 · Continue steps 1, 2, 3 and add each of these rhythms on the Snare Drum:

STEP 6 · Continue steps 1, 2, 3 and play this 8-bar exercise on the Snare Drum:

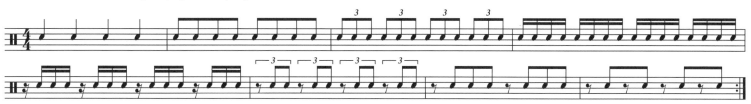

LESSON 1.11

STEP 1 · Start by playing either of these ostinatos on the Hi-Hat Foot:

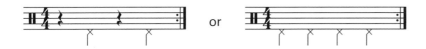

STEP 2 · Continue step 1 and add one of these ostinatos on the Bass Drum:

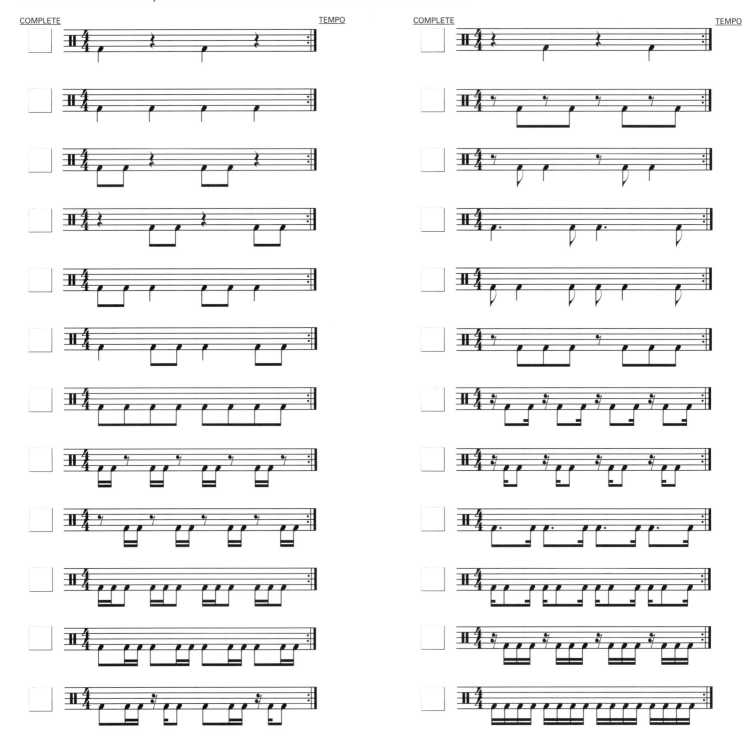

STEP 3 · Continue steps 1, 2 and add this ostinato on the Ride Cymbal:

STEP 4 · Continue steps 1, 2, 3 and add each of these rhythms on the Snare Drum:

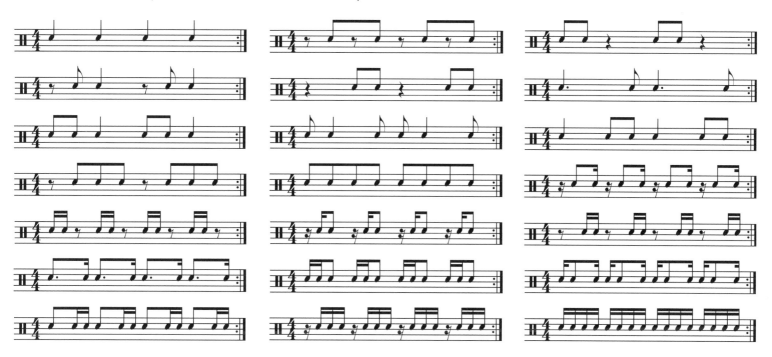

STEP 5 · Continue steps 1, 2, 3 and add each of these rhythms on the Snare Drum:

STEP 6 · Continue steps 1, 2, 3 and play this 8-bar exercise on the Snare Drum:

LESSON 1.12

STEP 1 · Start by playing either of these ostinatos on the Hi-Hat Foot:

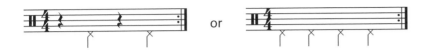

STEP 2 · Continue step 1 and add one of these ostinatos on the Bass Drum:

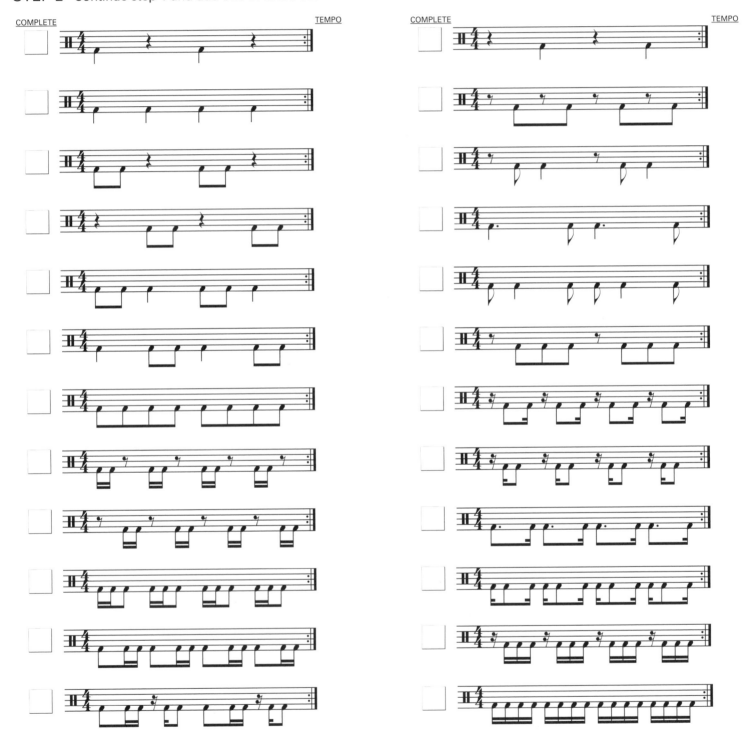

STEP 3 · Continue steps 1, 2 and add this ostinato on the Ride Cymbal:

STEP 4 · Continue steps 1, 2, 3 and add each of these rhythms on the Snare Drum:

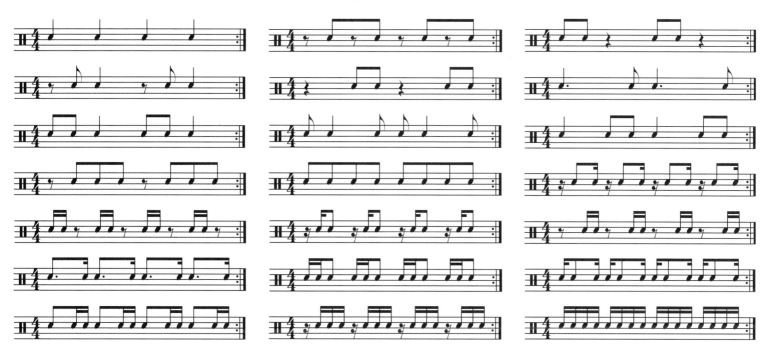

STEP 5 · Continue steps 1, 2, 3 and add each of these rhythms on the Snare Drum:

STEP 6 · Continue steps 1, 2, 3 and play this 8-bar exercise on the Snare Drum:

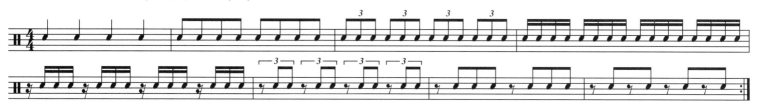

LESSON 1.13

STEP 1 · Start by playing either of these ostinatos on the Hi-Hat Foot:

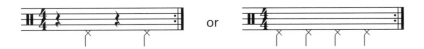

or

STEP 2 · Continue step 1 and add one of these ostinatos on the Bass Drum:

STEP 3 · Continue steps 1, 2 and add this ostinato on the Ride Cymbal:

STEP 4 · Continue steps 1, 2, 3 and add each of these rhythms on the Snare Drum:

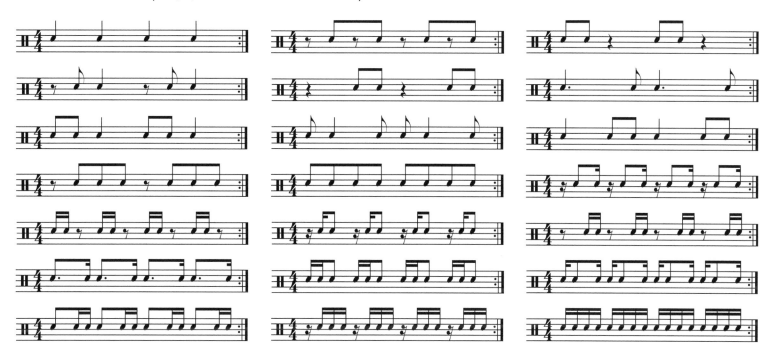

STEP 5 · Continue steps 1, 2, 3 and add each of these rhythms on the Snare Drum:

STEP 6 · Continue steps 1, 2, 3 and play this 8-bar exercise on the Snare Drum:

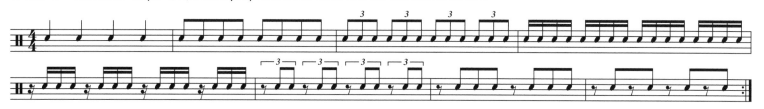

LESSON 1.14

STEP 1 · Start by playing either of these ostinatos on the Hi-Hat Foot:

STEP 2 · Continue step 1 and add one of these ostinatos on the Bass Drum:

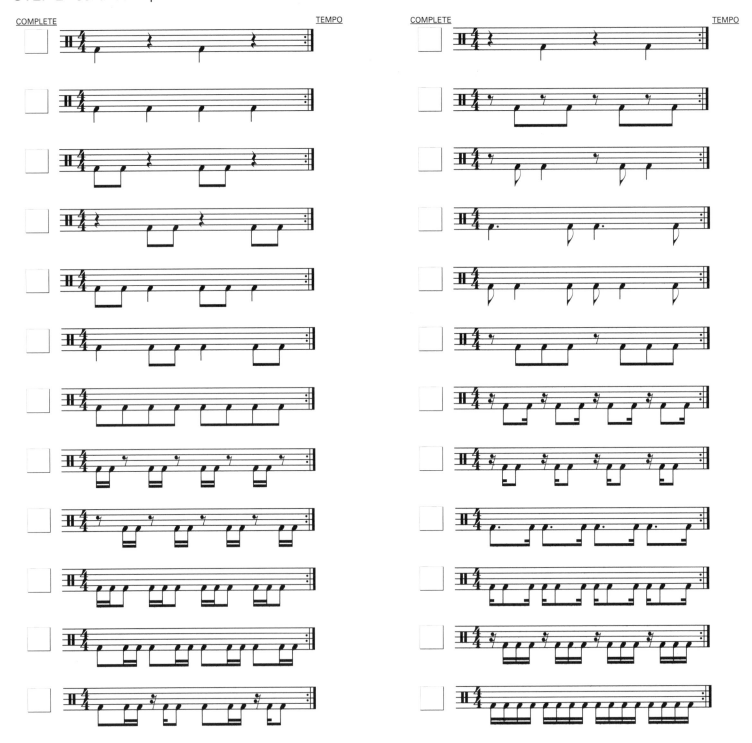

STEP 3 · Continue steps 1, 2 and add this ostinato on the Ride Cymbal:

STEP 4 · Continue steps 1, 2, 3 and add each of these rhythms on the Snare Drum:

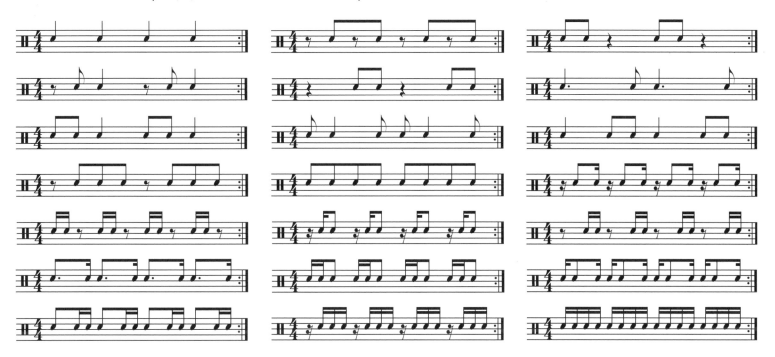

STEP 5 · Continue steps 1, 2, 3 and add each of these rhythms on the Snare Drum:

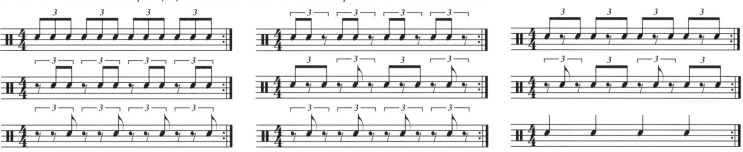

STEP 6 · Continue steps 1, 2, 3 and play this 8-bar exercise on the Snare Drum:

LESSON 1.15

30

STEP 1 · Start by playing either of these ostinatos on the Hi-Hat Foot:

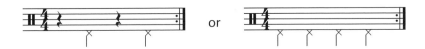

STEP 2 · Continue step 1 and add one of these ostinatos on the Bass Drum:

STEP 3 · Continue steps 1, 2 and add this ostinato on the Ride Cymbal:

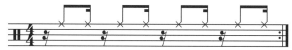

STEP 4 · Continue steps 1, 2, 3 and add each of these rhythms on the Snare Drum:

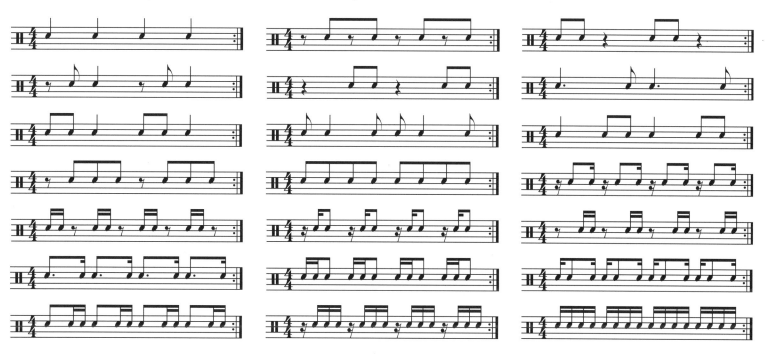

STEP 5 · Continue steps 1, 2, 3 and add each of these rhythms on the Snare Drum:

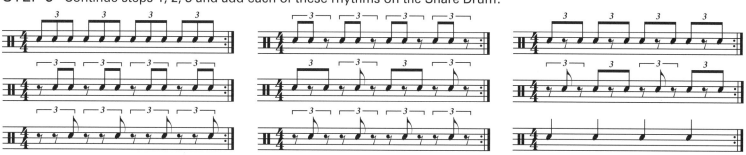

STEP 6 · Continue steps 1, 2, 3 and play this 8-bar exercise on the Snare Drum:

LESSON 1.16

STEP 1 · Start by playing either of these ostinatos on the Hi-Hat Foot:

STEP 2 · Continue step 1 and add one of these ostinatos on the Bass Drum:

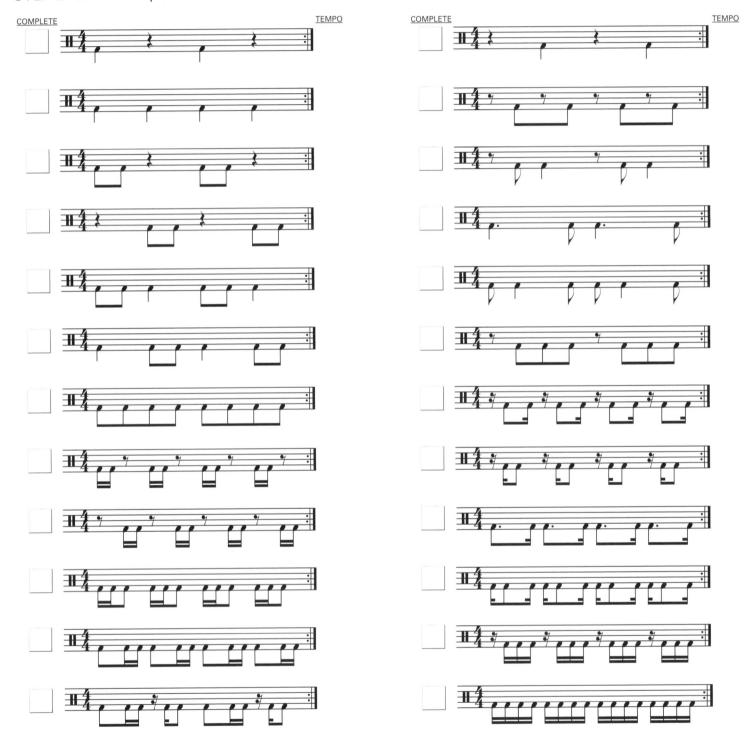

32

STEP 3 · Continue steps 1, 2 and add this ostinato on the Ride Cymbal:

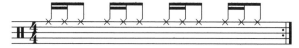

STEP 4 · Continue steps 1, 2, 3 and add each of these rhythms on the Snare Drum:

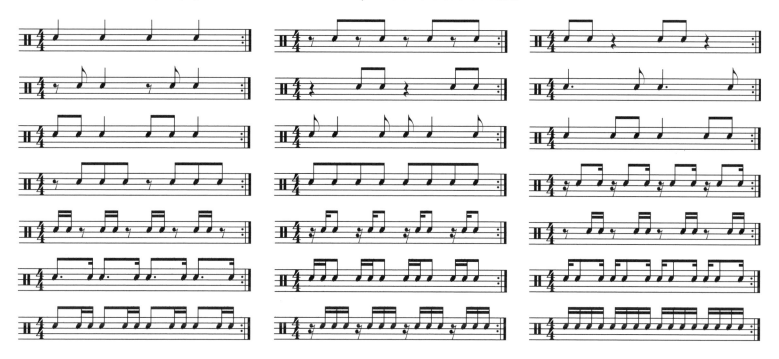

STEP 5 · Continue steps 1, 2, 3 and add each of these rhythms on the Snare Drum:

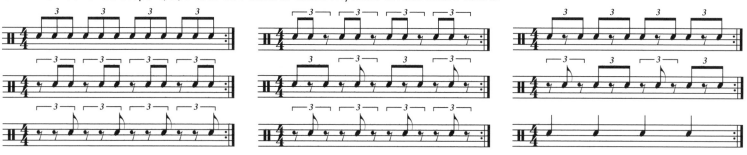

STEP 6 · Continue steps 1, 2, 3 and play this 8-bar exercise on the Snare Drum:

LESSON 1.17

STEP 1 · Start by playing either of these ostinatos on the Hi-Hat Foot:

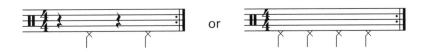

STEP 2 · Continue step 1 and add one of these ostinatos on the Bass Drum:

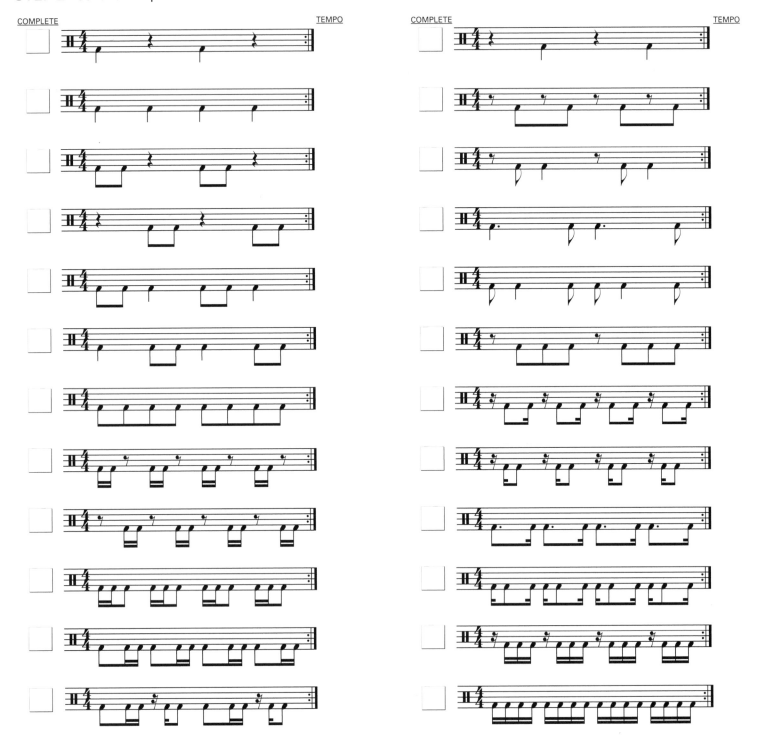

STEP 3 · Continue steps 1, 2 and add this ostinato on the Ride Cymbal:

STEP 4 · Continue steps 1, 2, 3 and add each of these rhythms on the Snare Drum:

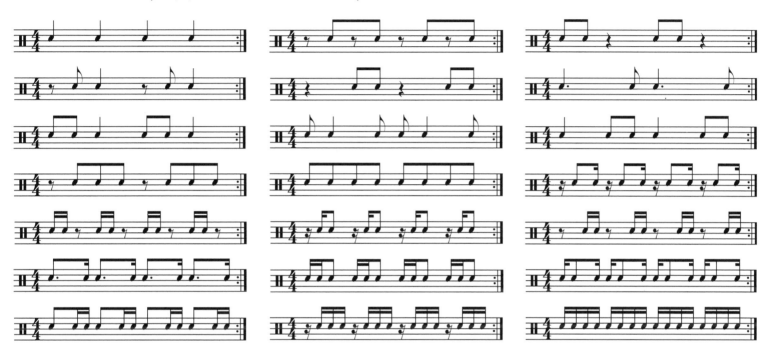

STEP 5 · Continue steps 1, 2, 3 and add each of these rhythms on the Snare Drum:

STEP 6 · Continue steps 1, 2, 3 and play this 8-bar exercise on the Snare Drum:

LESSON 1.18

STEP 1 · Start by playing either of these ostinatos on the Hi-Hat Foot:

STEP 2 · Continue step 1 and add one of these ostinatos on the Bass Drum:

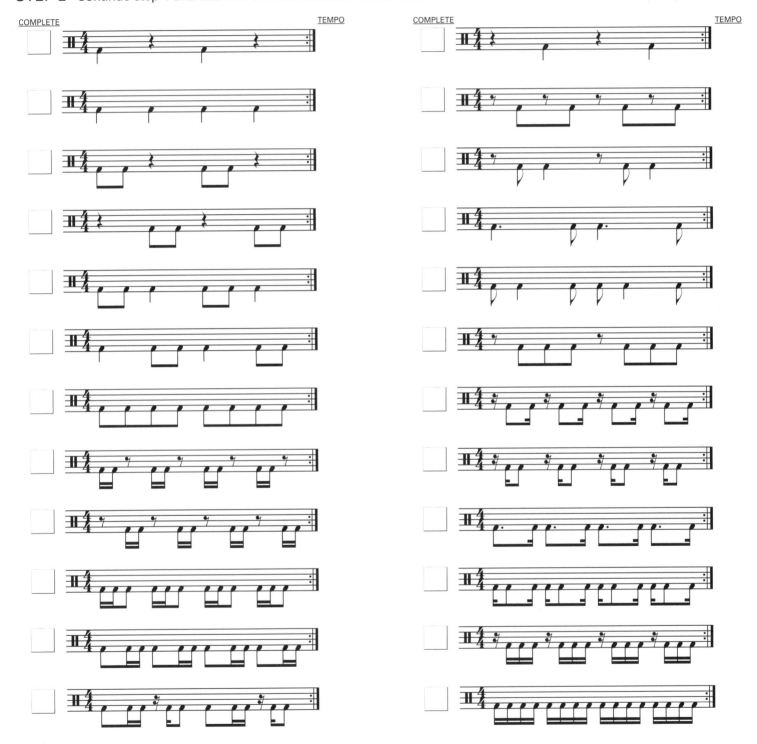

36

STEP 3 · Continue steps 1, 2 and add this ostinato on the Ride Cymbal:

STEP 4 · Continue steps 1, 2, 3 and add each of these rhythms on the Snare Drum:

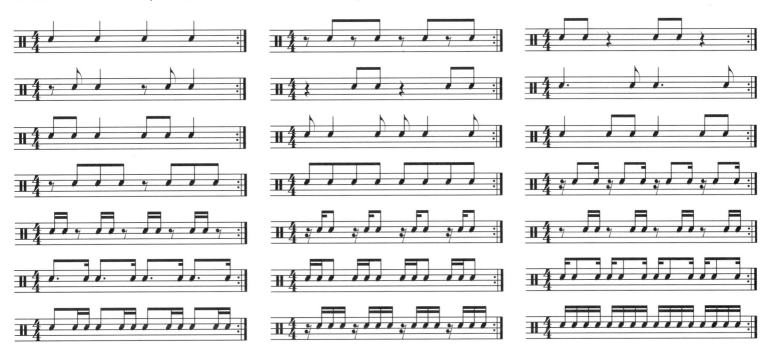

STEP 5 · Continue steps 1, 2, 3 and add each of these rhythms on the Snare Drum:

STEP 6 · Continue steps 1, 2, 3 and play this 8-bar exercise on the Snare Drum:

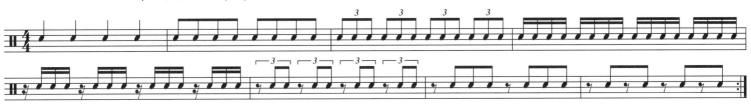

LESSON 1.19

STEP 1 · Start by playing either of these ostinatos on the Hi-Hat Foot:

STEP 2 · Continue step 1 and add one of these ostinatos on the Bass Drum:

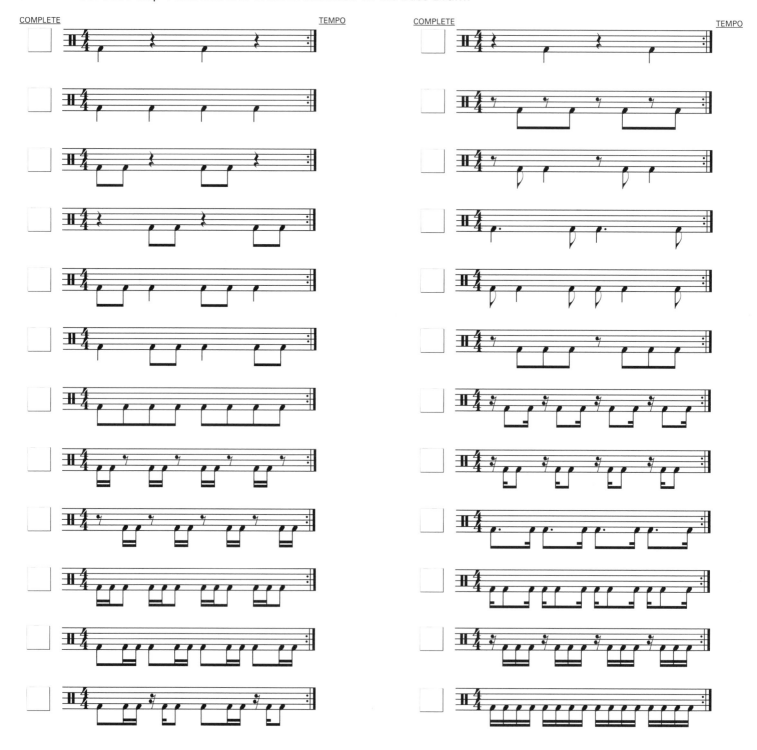

STEP 3 · Continue steps 1, 2 and add this ostinato on the Ride Cymbal:

STEP 4 · Continue steps 1, 2, 3 and add each of these rhythms on the Snare Drum:

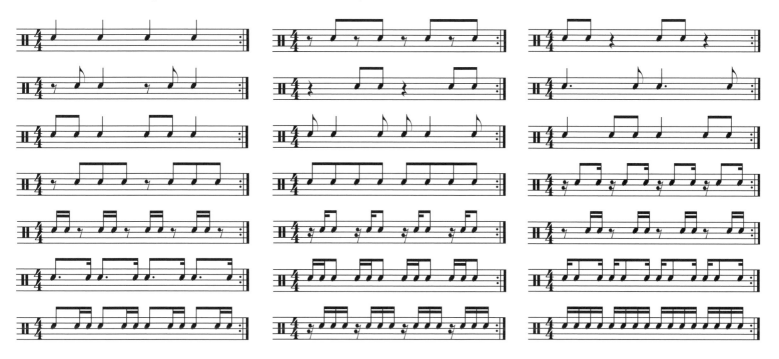

STEP 5 · Continue steps 1, 2, 3 and add each of these rhythms on the Snare Drum:

STEP 6 · Continue steps 1, 2, 3 and play this 8-bar exercise on the Snare Drum:

LESSON 1.20

STEP 1 · Start by playing either of these ostinatos on the Hi-Hat Foot:

STEP 2 · Continue step 1 and add one of these ostinatos on the Bass Drum:

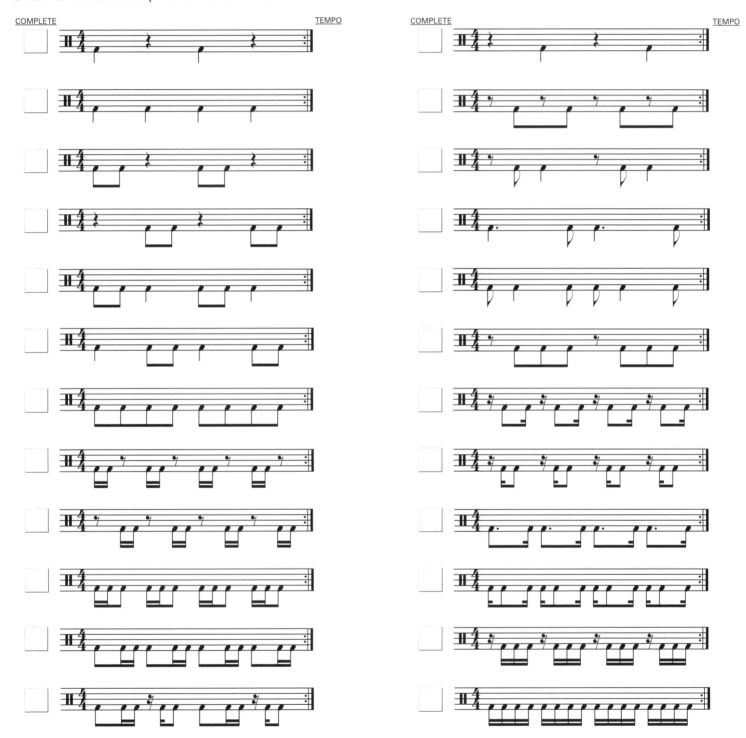

STEP 3 · Continue steps 1, 2 and add this ostinato on the Ride Cymbal:

STEP 4 · Continue steps 1, 2, 3 and add each of these rhythms on the Snare Drum:

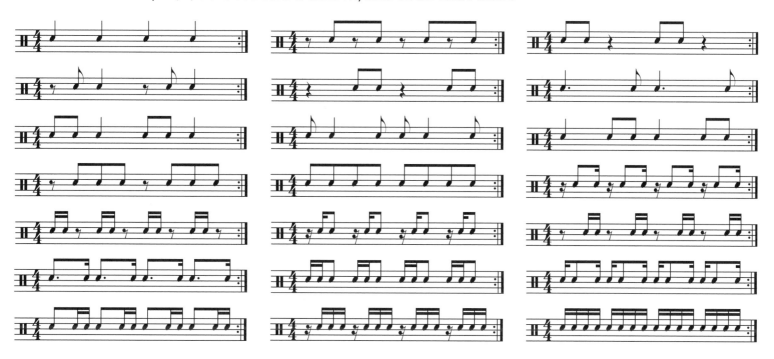

STEP 5 · Continue steps 1, 2, 3 and add each of these rhythms on the Snare Drum:

STEP 6 · Continue steps 1, 2, 3 and play this 8-bar exercise on the Snare Drum:

LESSON 1.21

STEP 1 · Start by playing either of these ostinatos on the Hi-Hat Foot:

STEP 2 · Continue step 1 and add one of these ostinatos on the Bass Drum:

STEP 3 · Continue steps 1, 2 and add this ostinato on the Ride Cymbal:

STEP 4 · Continue steps 1, 2, 3 and add each of these rhythms on the Snare Drum:

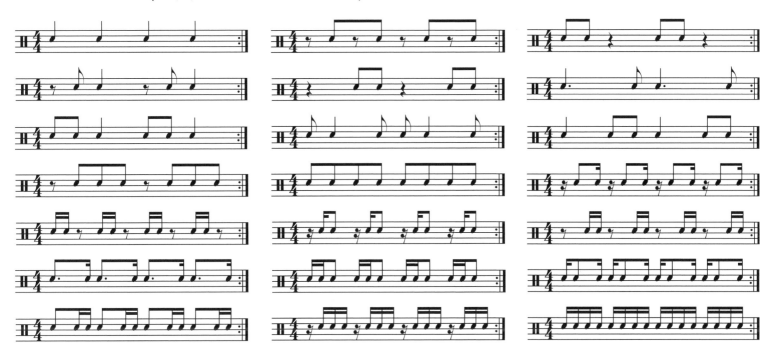

STEP 5 · Continue steps 1, 2, 3 and add each of these rhythms on the Snare Drum:

STEP 6 · Continue steps 1, 2, 3 and play this 8-bar exercise on the Snare Drum:

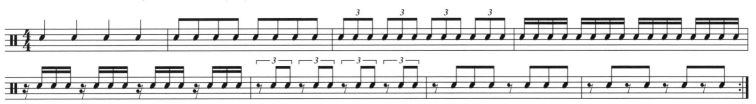

LESSON 1.22

STEP 1 · Start by playing either of these ostinatos on the Hi-Hat Foot:

STEP 2 · Continue step 1 and add one of these ostinatos on the Bass Drum:

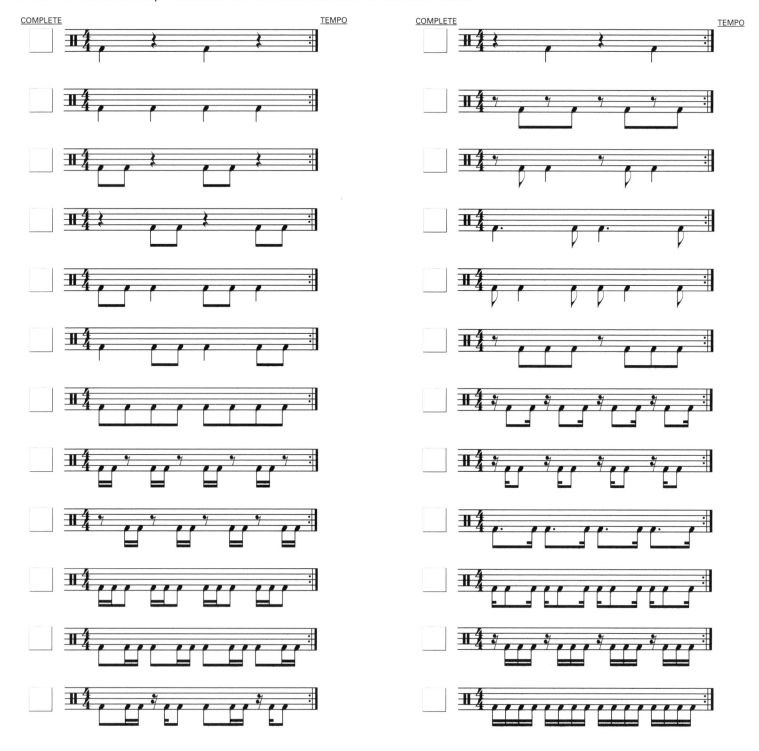

44

STEP 3 · Continue steps 1, 2 and add this ostinato on the Ride Cymbal:

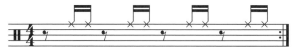

STEP 4 · Continue steps 1, 2, 3 and add each of these rhythms on the Snare Drum:

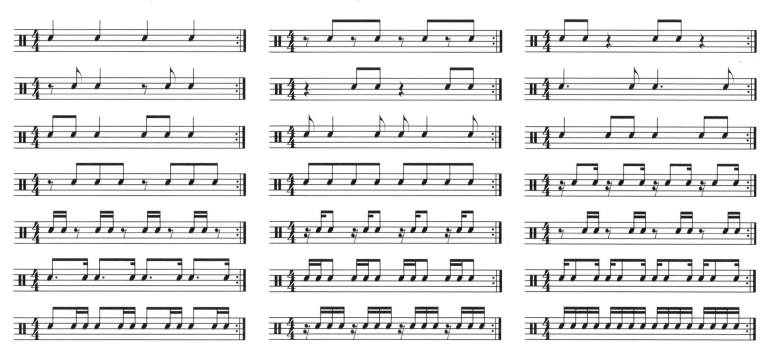

STEP 5 · Continue steps 1, 2, 3 and add each of these rhythms on the Snare Drum:

STEP 6 · Continue steps 1, 2, 3 and play this 8-bar exercise on the Snare Drum:

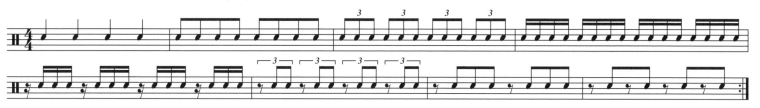

LESSON 1.23

STEP 1 · Start by playing either of these ostinatos on the Hi-Hat Foot:

STEP 2 · Continue step 1 and add one of these ostinatos on the Bass Drum:

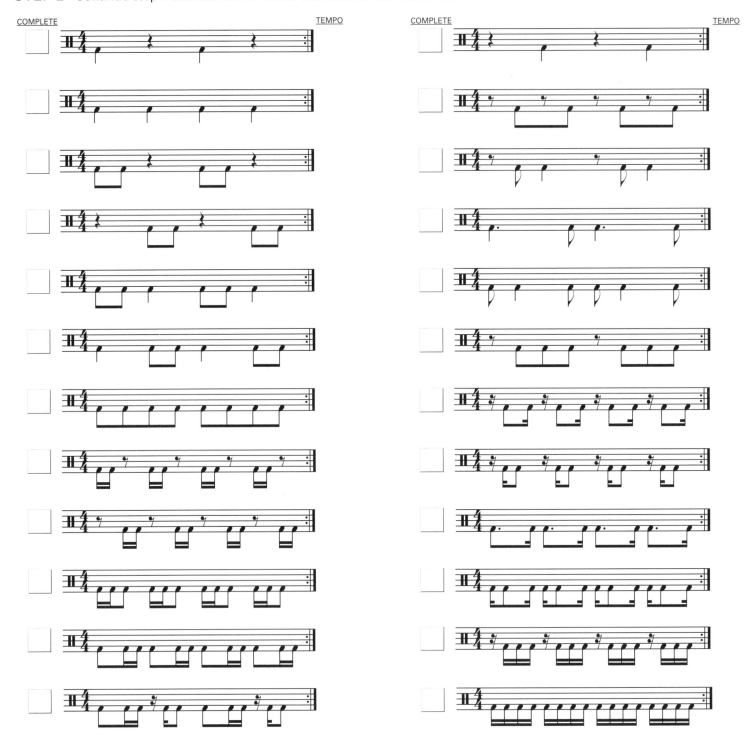

STEP 3 · Continue steps 1, 2 and add this ostinato on the Ride Cymbal:

STEP 4 · Continue steps 1, 2, 3 and add each of these rhythms on the Snare Drum:

STEP 5 · Continue steps 1, 2, 3 and add each of these rhythms on the Snare Drum:

STEP 6 · Continue steps 1, 2, 3 and play this 8-bar exercise on the Snare Drum:

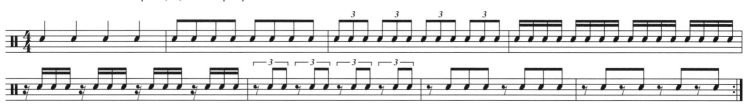

LESSON 1.24

STEP 1 · Start by playing either of these ostinatos on the Hi-Hat Foot:

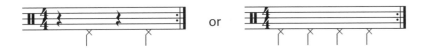

STEP 2 · Continue step 1 and add one of these ostinatos on the Bass Drum:

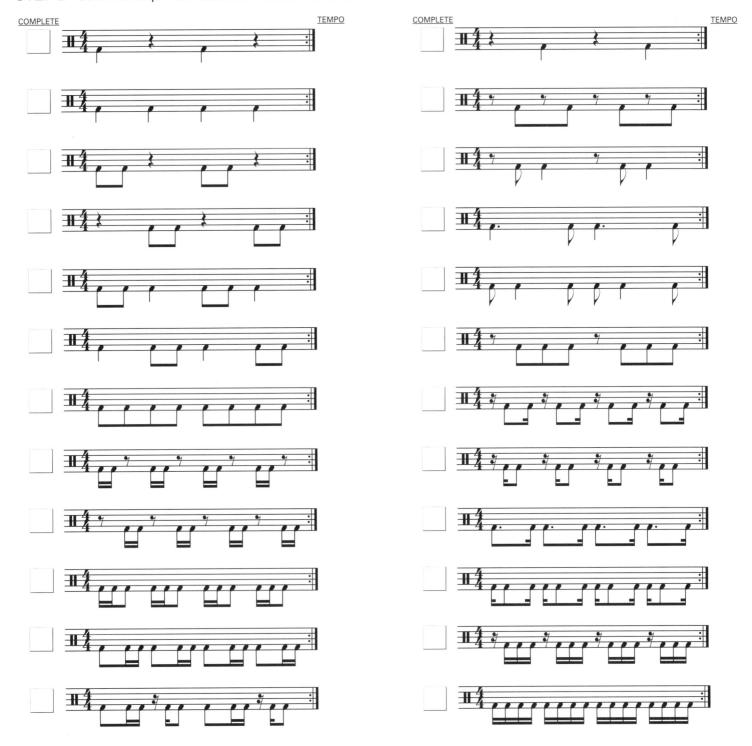

STEP 3 · Continue steps 1, 2 and add this ostinato on the Ride Cymbal:

STEP 4 · Continue steps 1, 2, 3 and add each of these rhythms on the Snare Drum:

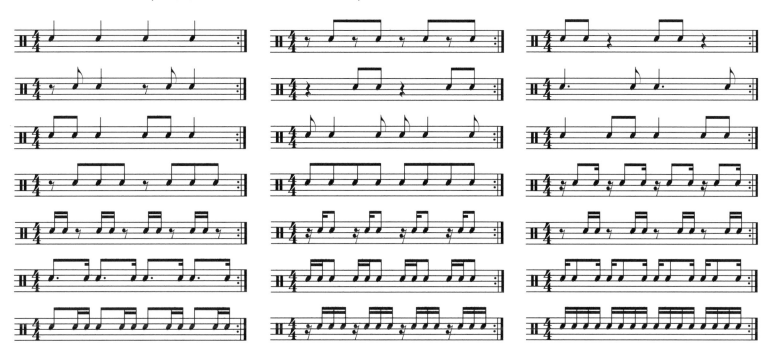

STEP 5 · Continue steps 1, 2, 3 and add each of these rhythms on the Snare Drum:

STEP 6 · Continue steps 1, 2, 3 and play this 8-bar exercise on the Snare Drum:

HI-HAT FOOT & VOCAL RHYTHMS

Additional Ostinatos for Use with Section One

Pick a lesson you've completed and replace Step 1 with one of these Hi-Hat Foot rhythms. Play through the lesson as written, including multiple variations of Step 2. When complete, pick another Hi-Hat Foot ostinato to try. Focus on balance and take it slowly as these can be quite challenging.

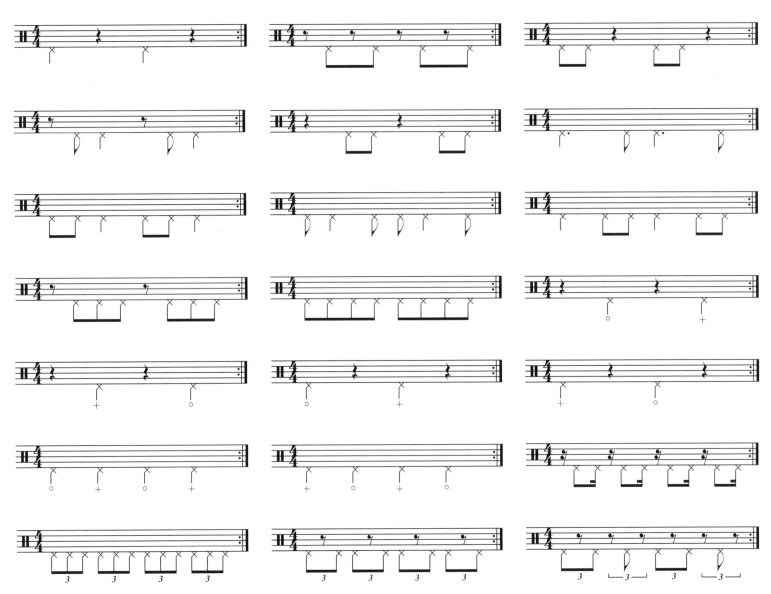

Pick a lesson you've completed and count one of these Vocal rhythms out loud. Play through the lesson as written, including multiple variations of Step 2. When complete, pick another Vocal ostinato to try. Keep your voice even and focus to make it rhythmically independent from your hands and feet.

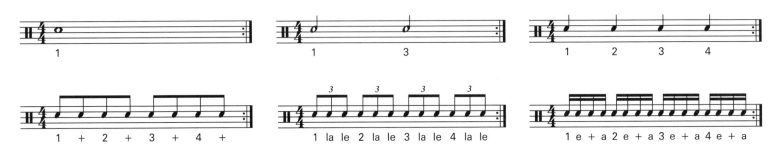

SECTION TWO
BLUES • JAZZ • 12/8 • 6/8

LESSON 2.1

STEP 1 · Start by playing either of these ostinatos on the Hi-Hat Foot:

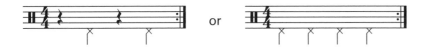

STEP 2 · Continue step 1 and add one of these ostinatos on the Bass Drum:

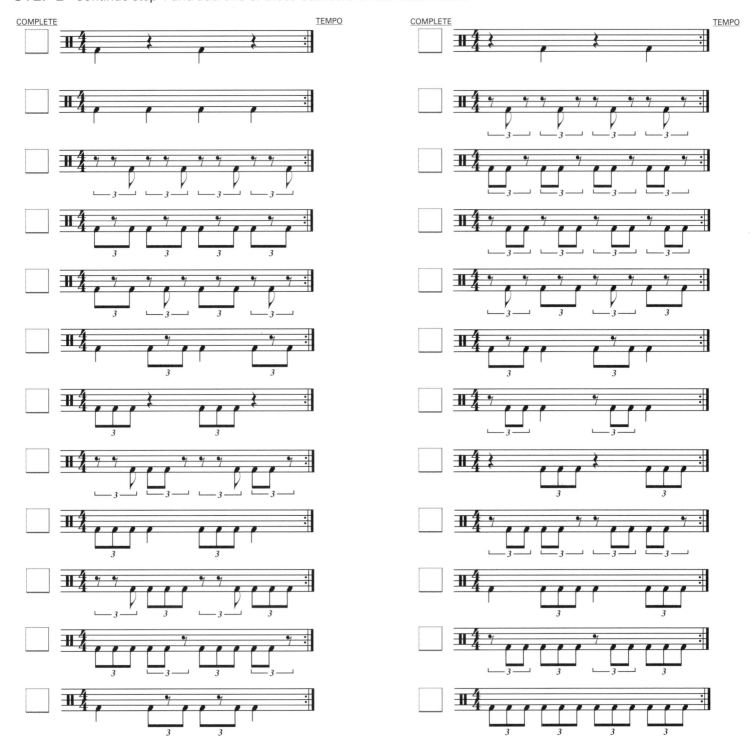

STEP 3 · Continue steps 1, 2 and add this ostinato on the Ride Cymbal:

STEP 4 · Continue steps 1, 2, 3 and add each of these rhythms on the Snare Drum:

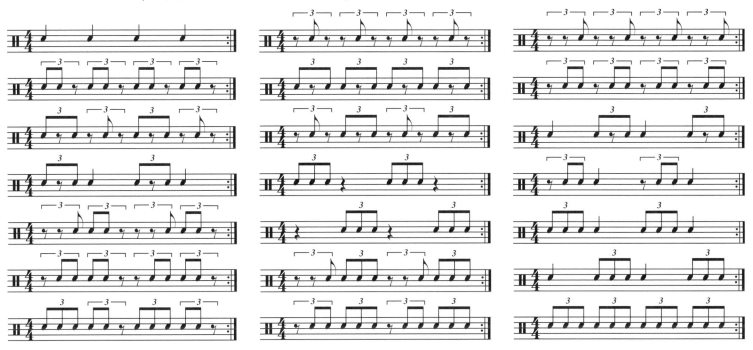

STEP 5 · Continue steps 1, 2, 3 and add each of these rhythms on the Snare Drum:

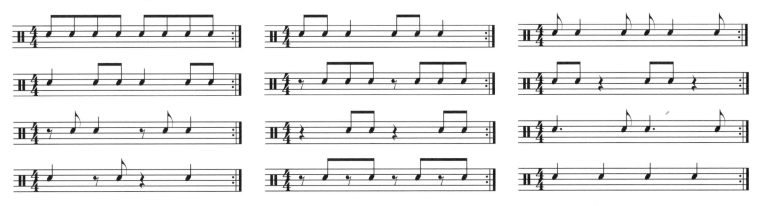

STEP 6 · Continue steps 1, 2, 3 and play this 6-bar exercise on the Snare Drum:

LESSON 2.2

STEP 1 · Start by playing either of these ostinatos on the Hi-Hat Foot:

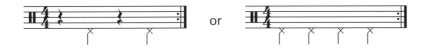

STEP 2 · Continue step 1 and add one of these ostinatos on the Bass Drum:

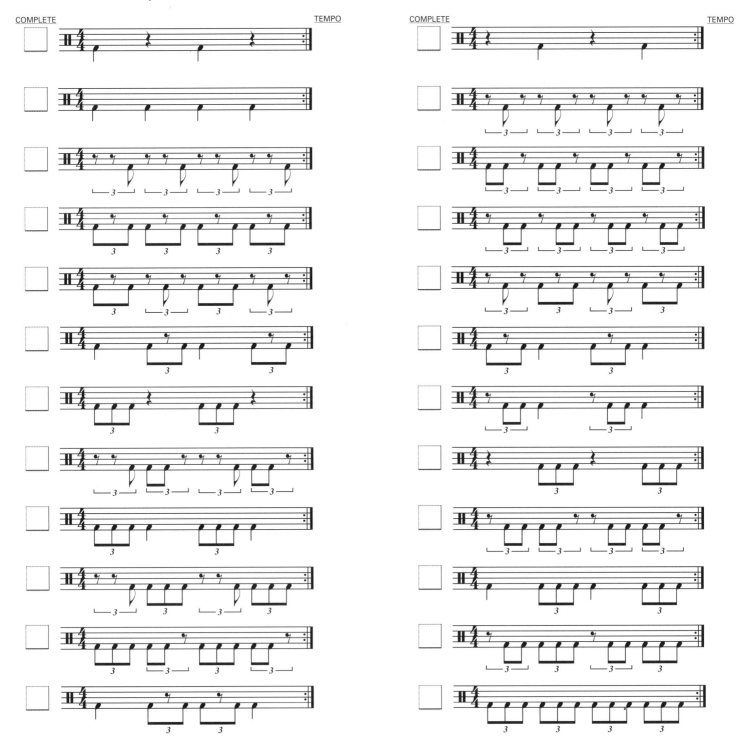

STEP 3 · Continue steps 1, 2 and add this ostinato on the Ride Cymbal:

STEP 4 · Continue steps 1, 2, 3 and add each of these rhythms on the Snare Drum:

STEP 5 · Continue steps 1, 2, 3 and add each of these rhythms on the Snare Drum:

STEP 6 · Continue steps 1, 2, 3 and play this 6-bar exercise on the Snare Drum:

LESSON 2.3

STEP 1 · Start by playing either of these ostinatos on the Hi-Hat Foot:

STEP 2 · Continue step 1 and add one of these ostinatos on the Bass Drum:

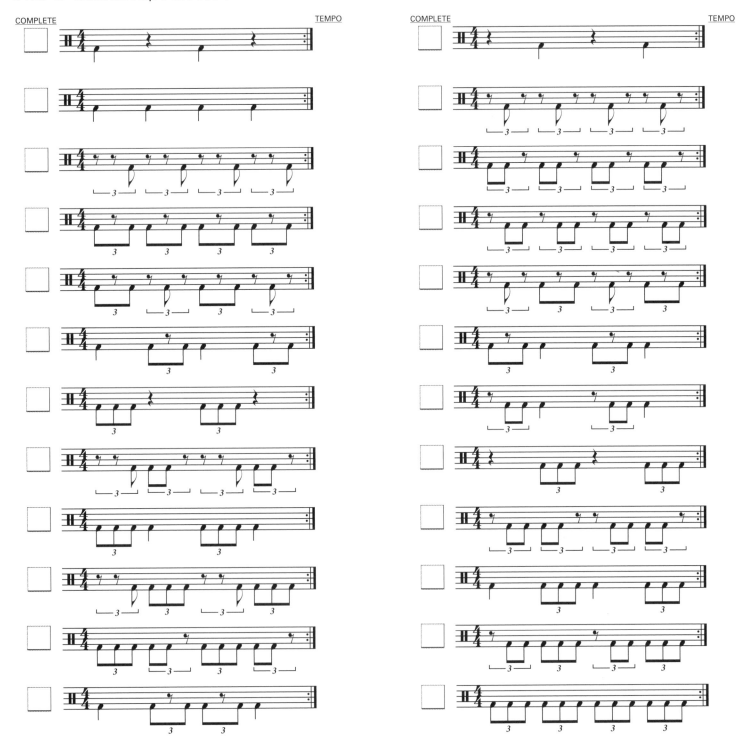

STEP 3 · Continue steps 1, 2 and add this ostinato on the Ride Cymbal:

STEP 4 · Continue steps 1, 2, 3 and add each of these rhythms on the Snare Drum:

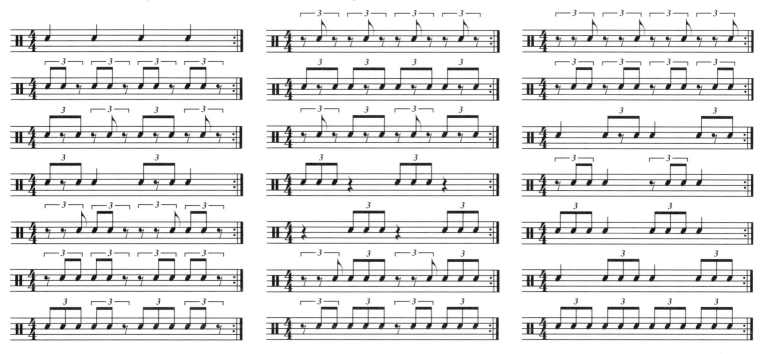

STEP 5 · Continue steps 1, 2, 3 and add each of these rhythms on the Snare Drum:

STEP 6 · Continue steps 1, 2, 3 and play this 6-bar exercise on the Snare Drum:

LESSON 2.4

STEP 1 · Start by playing either of these ostinatos on the Hi-Hat Foot:

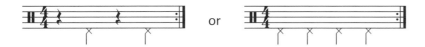

or

STEP 2 · Continue step 1 and add one of these ostinatos on the Bass Drum:

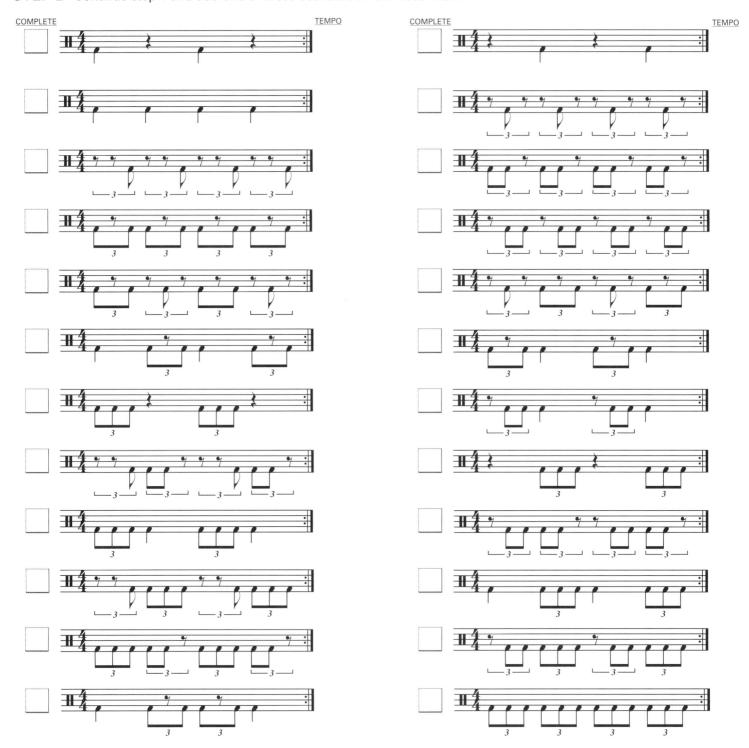

STEP 3 · Continue steps 1, 2 and add this ostinato on the Ride Cymbal:

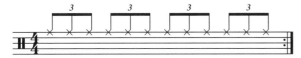

STEP 4 · Continue steps 1, 2, 3 and add each of these rhythms on the Snare Drum:

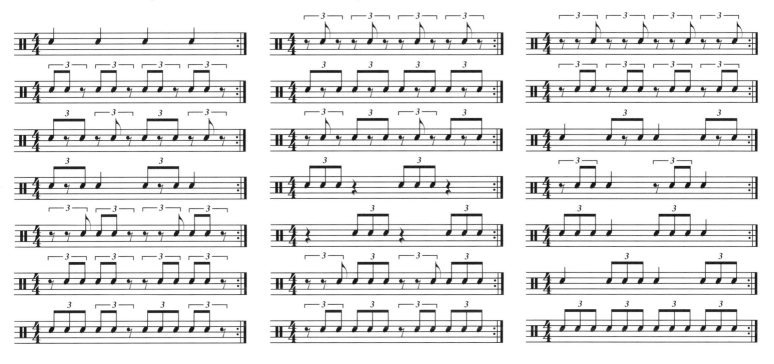

STEP 5 · Continue steps 1, 2, 3 and add each of these rhythms on the Snare Drum:

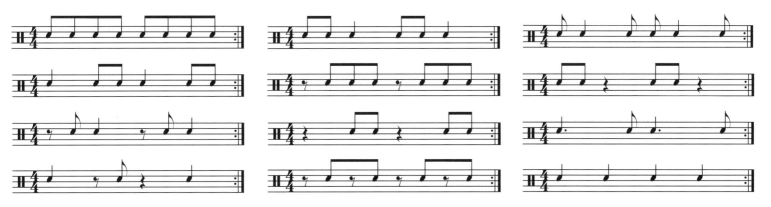

STEP 6 · Continue steps 1, 2, 3 and play this 6-bar exercise on the Snare Drum:

LESSON 2.5

STEP 1 · Start by playing either of these ostinatos on the Hi-Hat Foot:

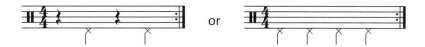

STEP 2 · Continue step 1 and add one of these ostinatos on the Bass Drum:

STEP 3 · Continue steps 1, 2 and add this ostinato on the Ride Cymbal:

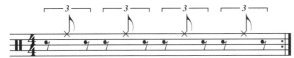

STEP 4 · Continue steps 1, 2, 3 and add each of these rhythms on the Snare Drum:

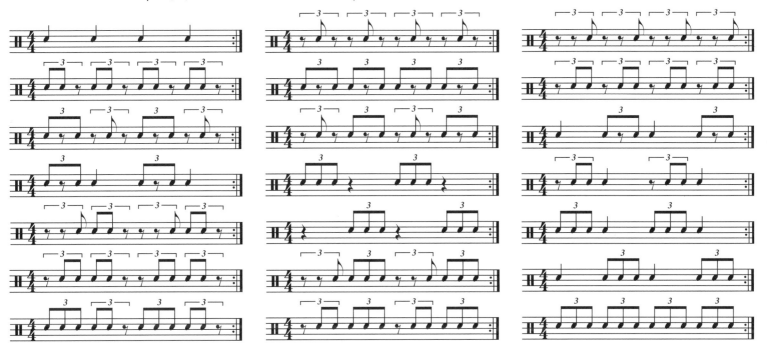

STEP 5 · Continue steps 1, 2, 3 and add each of these rhythms on the Snare Drum:

STEP 6 · Continue steps 1, 2, 3 and play this 6-bar exercise on the Snare Drum:

LESSON 2.6

STEP 1 · Start by playing either of these ostinatos on the Hi-Hat Foot:

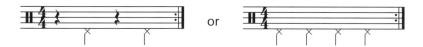

STEP 2 · Continue step 1 and add one of these ostinatos on the Bass Drum:

STEP 3 · Continue steps 1, 2 and add this ostinato on the Ride Cymbal:

STEP 4 · Continue steps 1, 2, 3 and add each of these rhythms on the Snare Drum:

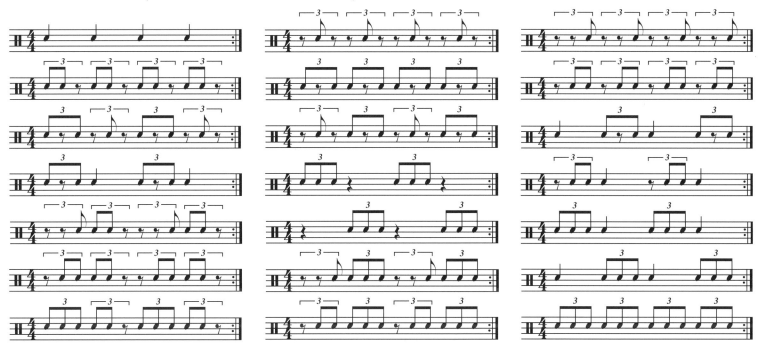

STEP 5 · Continue steps 1, 2, 3 and add each of these rhythms on the Snare Drum:

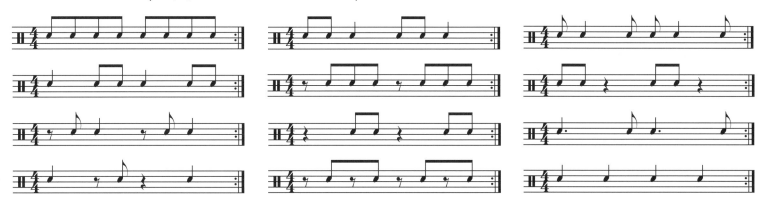

STEP 6 · Continue steps 1, 2, 3 and play this 6-bar exercise on the Snare Drum:

LESSON 2.7

STEP 1 · Start by playing either of these ostinatos on the Hi-Hat Foot:

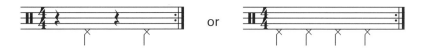

STEP 2 · Continue step 1 and add one of these ostinatos on the Bass Drum:

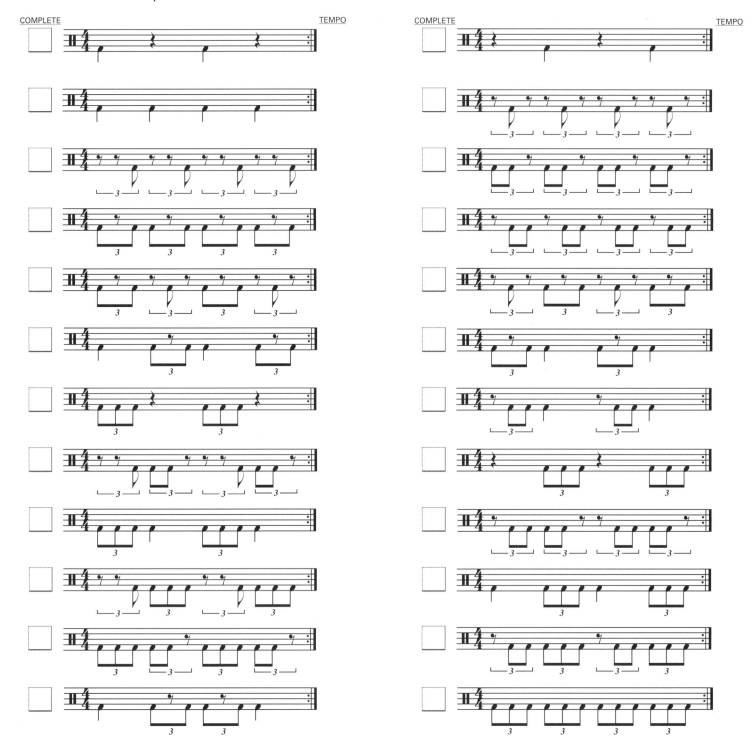

STEP 3 · Continue steps 1, 2 and add this ostinato on the Ride Cymbal:

STEP 4 · Continue steps 1, 2, 3 and add each of these rhythms on the Snare Drum:

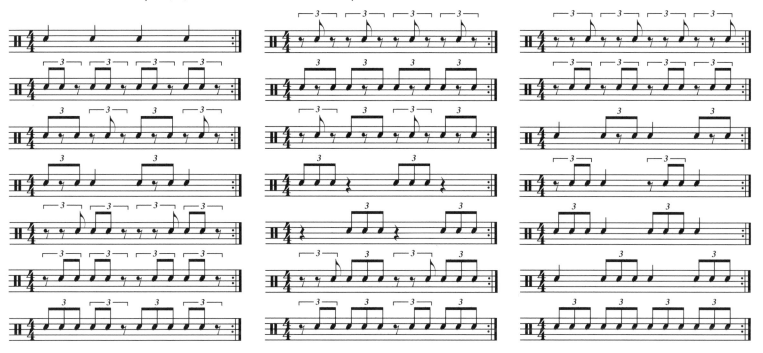

STEP 5 · Continue steps 1, 2, 3 and add each of these rhythms on the Snare Drum:

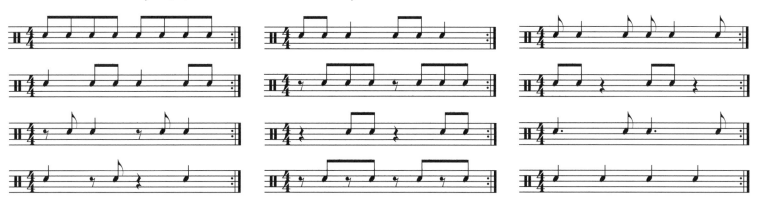

STEP 6 · Continue steps 1, 2, 3 and play this 6-bar exercise on the Snare Drum:

LESSON 2.8

STEP 1 · Start by playing either of these ostinatos on the Hi-Hat Foot:

STEP 2 · Continue step 1 and add one of these ostinatos on the Bass Drum:

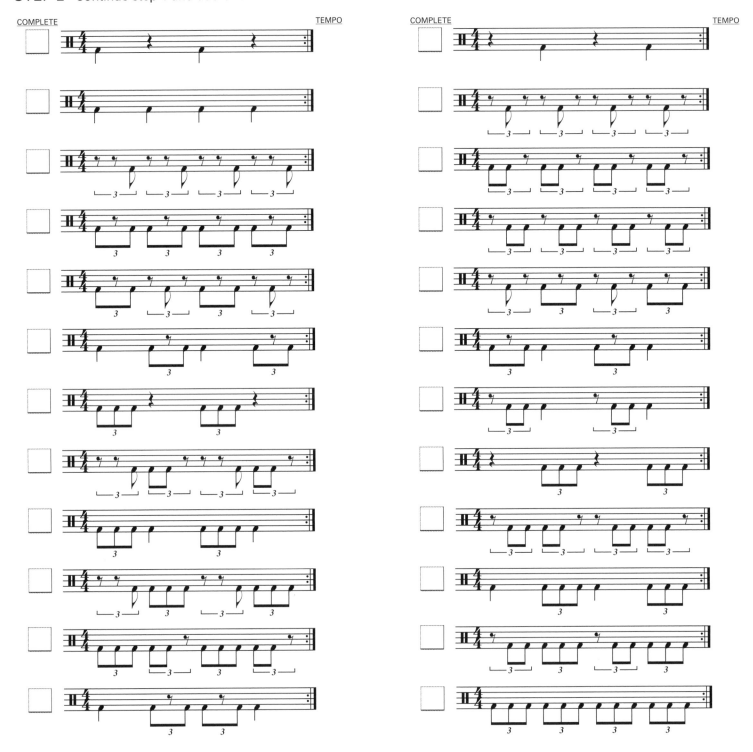

STEP 3 · Continue steps 1, 2 and add this ostinato on the Ride Cymbal:

STEP 4 · Continue steps 1, 2, 3 and add each of these rhythms on the Snare Drum:

STEP 5 · Continue steps 1, 2, 3 and add each of these rhythms on the Snare Drum:

STEP 6 · Continue steps 1, 2, 3 and play this 6-bar exercise on the Snare Drum:

LESSON 2.9

STEP 1 · Start by playing either of these ostinatos on the Hi-Hat Foot:

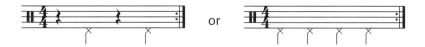

STEP 2 · Continue step 1 and add one of these ostinatos on the Bass Drum:

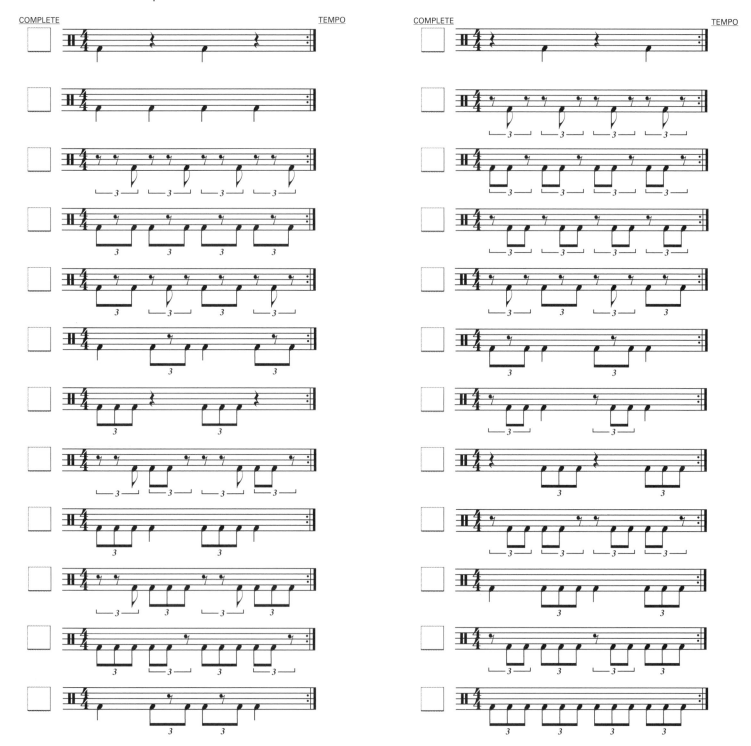

STEP 3 · Continue steps 1, 2 and add this ostinato on the Ride Cymbal:

STEP 4 · Continue steps 1, 2, 3 and add each of these rhythms on the Snare Drum:

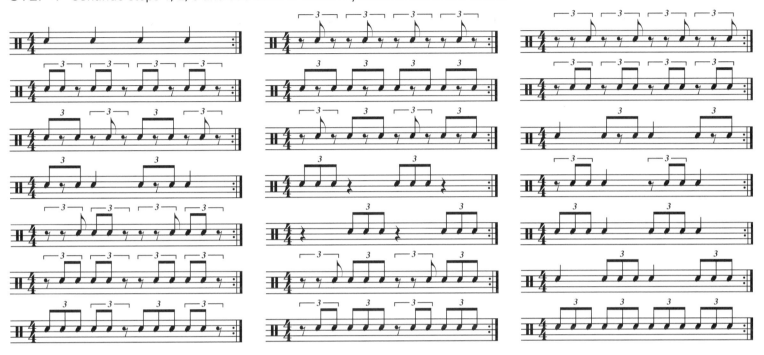

STEP 5 · Continue steps 1, 2, 3 and add each of these rhythms on the Snare Drum:

STEP 6 · Continue steps 1, 2, 3 and play this 6-bar exercise on the Snare Drum:

LESSON 2.10

STEP 1 · Start by playing either of these ostinatos on the Hi-Hat Foot:

STEP 2 · Continue step 1 and add one of these ostinatos on the Bass Drum:

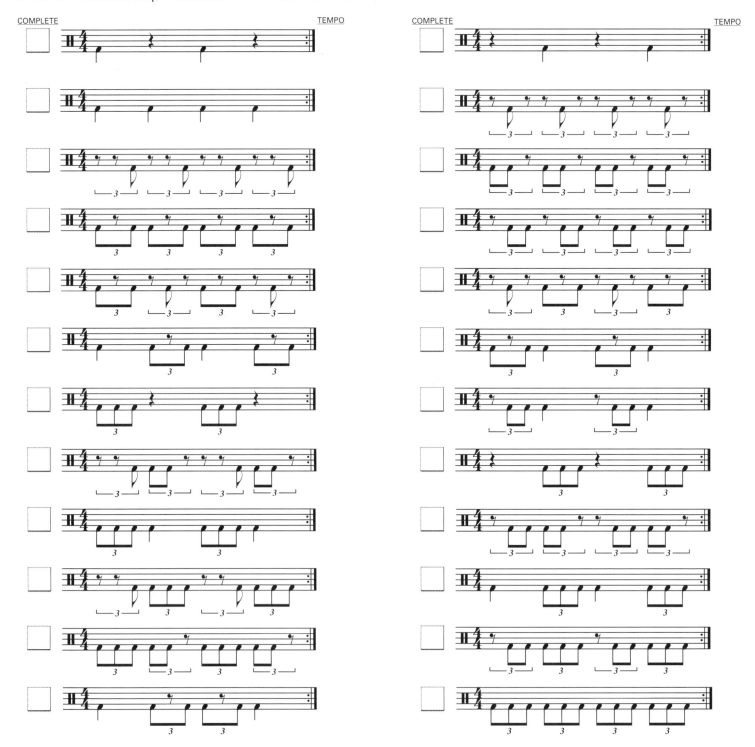

STEP 3 · Continue steps 1, 2 and add this ostinato on the Ride Cymbal:

STEP 4 · Continue steps 1, 2, 3 and add each of these rhythms on the Snare Drum:

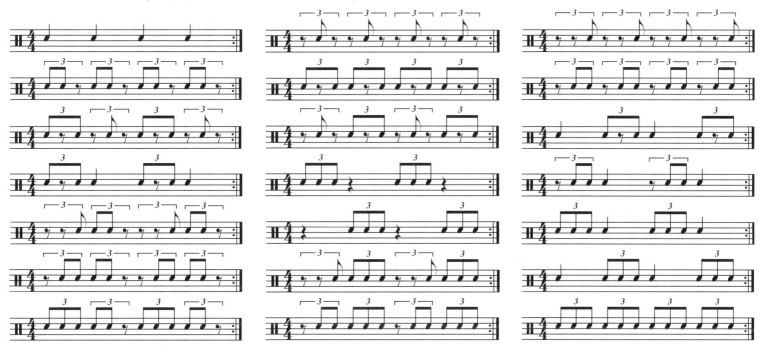

STEP 5 · Continue steps 1, 2, 3 and add each of these rhythms on the Snare Drum:

STEP 6 · Continue steps 1, 2, 3 and play this 6-bar exercise on the Snare Drum:

LESSON 2.11

STEP 1 · Start by playing either of these ostinatos on the Hi-Hat Foot:

STEP 2 · Continue step 1 and add one of these ostinatos on the Bass Drum:

STEP 3 · Continue steps 1, 2 and add this ostinato on the Ride Cymbal:

STEP 4 · Continue steps 1, 2, 3 and add each of these rhythms on the Snare Drum:

STEP 5 · Continue steps 1, 2, 3 and add each of these rhythms on the Snare Drum:

STEP 6 · Continue steps 1, 2, 3 and play this 6-bar exercise on the Snare Drum:

LESSON 2.12

STEP 1 · Start by playing either of these ostinatos on the Hi-Hat Foot:

STEP 2 · Continue step 1 and add one of these ostinatos on the Bass Drum:

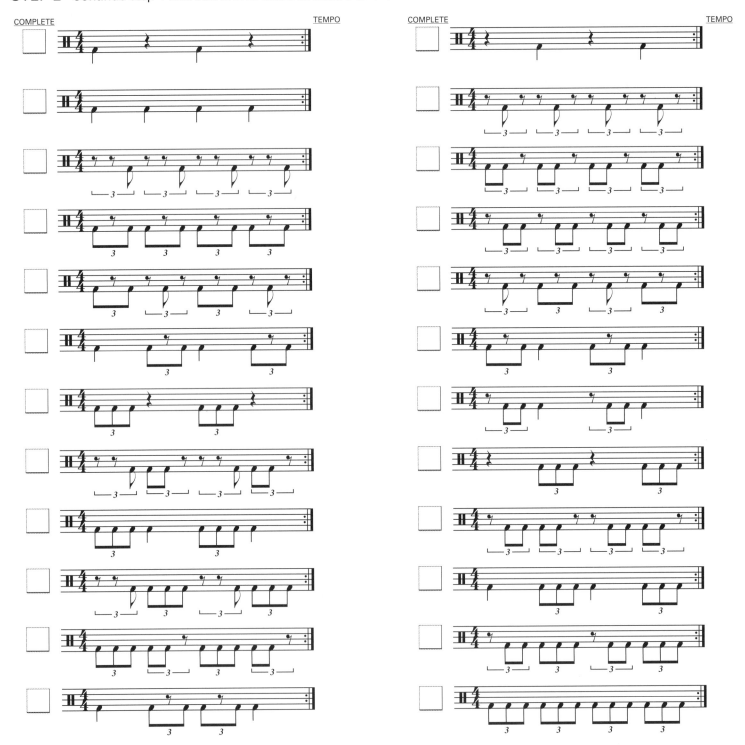

STEP 3 · Continue steps 1, 2 and add this ostinato on the Ride Cymbal:

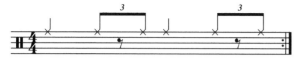

STEP 4 · Continue steps 1, 2, 3 and add each of these rhythms on the Snare Drum:

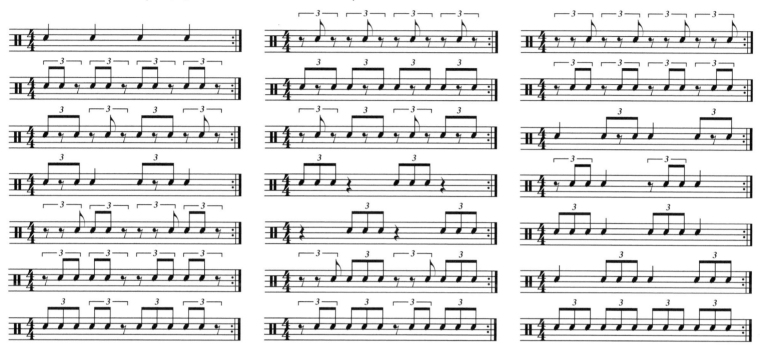

STEP 5 · Continue steps 1, 2, 3 and add each of these rhythms on the Snare Drum:

STEP 6 · Continue steps 1, 2, 3 and play this 6-bar exercise on the Snare Drum:

LESSON 2.13

STEP 1 · Start by playing either of these ostinatos on the Hi-Hat Foot:

STEP 2 · Continue step 1 and add one of these ostinatos on the Bass Drum:

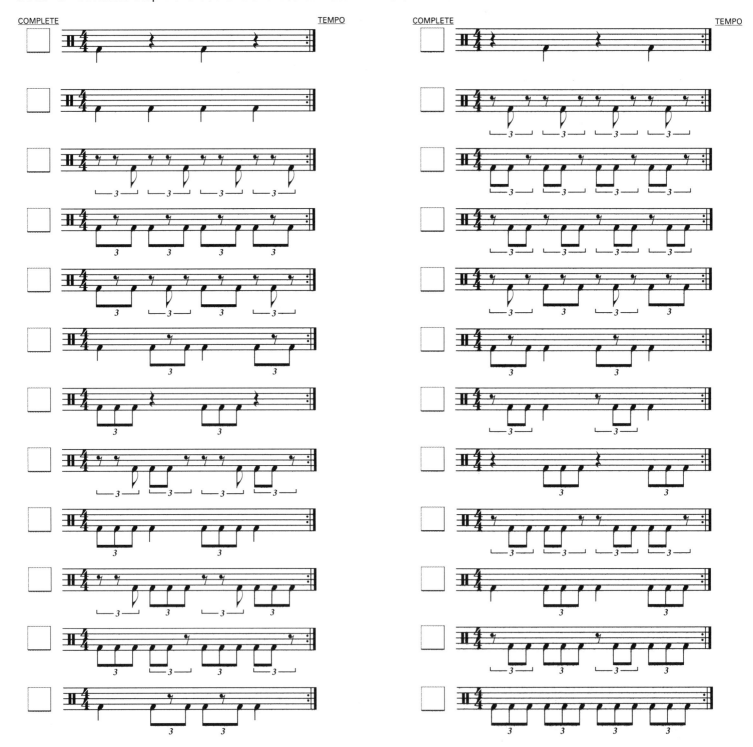

STEP 3 · Continue steps 1, 2 and add this ostinato on the Ride Cymbal:

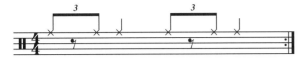

STEP 4 · Continue steps 1, 2, 3 and add each of these rhythms on the Snare Drum:

STEP 5 · Continue steps 1, 2, 3 and add each of these rhythms on the Snare Drum:

STEP 6 · Continue steps 1, 2, 3 and play this 6-bar exercise on the Snare Drum:

LESSON 2.14

STEP 1 · Start by playing either of these ostinatos on the Hi-Hat Foot:

STEP 2 · Continue step 1 and add one of these ostinatos on the Bass Drum:

STEP 3 · Continue steps 1, 2 and add this ostinato on the Ride Cymbal:

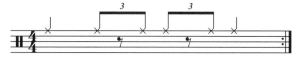

STEP 4 · Continue steps 1, 2, 3 and add each of these rhythms on the Snare Drum:

STEP 5 · Continue steps 1, 2, 3 and add each of these rhythms on the Snare Drum:

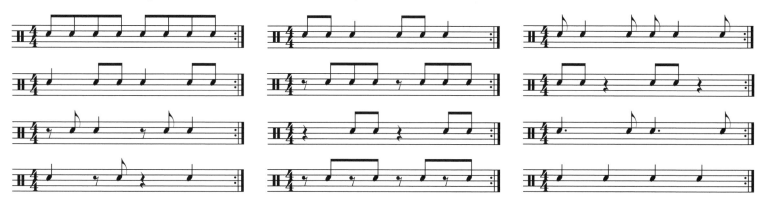

STEP 6 · Continue steps 1, 2, 3 and play this 6-bar exercise on the Snare Drum:

LESSON 2.15

STEP 1 · Start by playing either of these ostinatos on the Hi-Hat Foot:

STEP 2 · Continue step 1 and add one of these ostinatos on the Bass Drum:

STEP 3 · Continue steps 1, 2 and add this ostinato on the Ride Cymbal:

STEP 4 · Continue steps 1, 2, 3 and add each of these rhythms on the Snare Drum:

STEP 5 · Continue steps 1, 2, 3 and add each of these rhythms on the Snare Drum:

STEP 6 · Continue steps 1, 2, 3 and play this 6-bar exercise on the Snare Drum:

LESSON 2.16

STEP 1 · Start by playing either of these ostinatos on the Hi-Hat Foot:

STEP 2 · Continue step 1 and add one of these ostinatos on the Bass Drum:

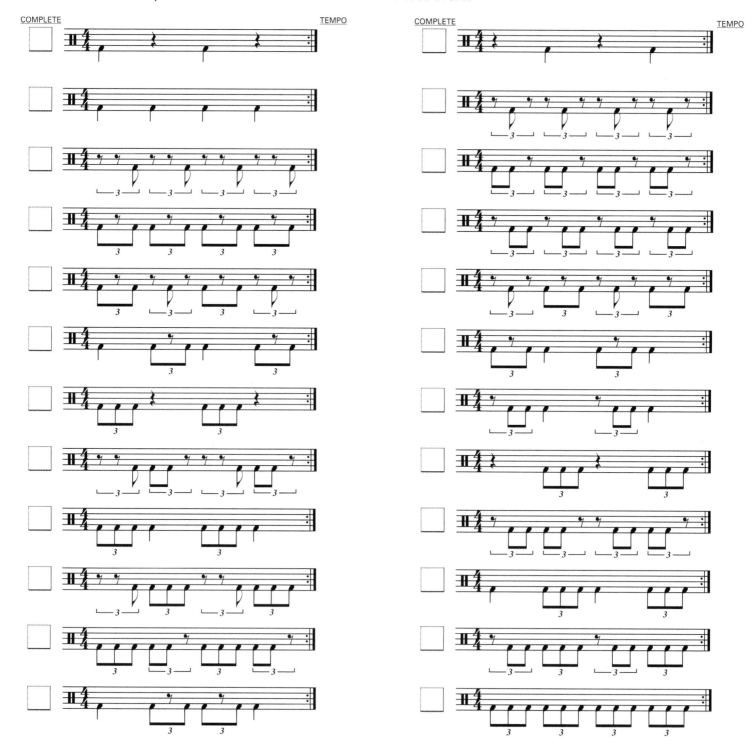

STEP 3 · Continue steps 1, 2 and add this ostinato on the Ride Cymbal:

STEP 4 · Continue steps 1, 2, 3 and add each of these rhythms on the Snare Drum:

STEP 5 · Continue steps 1, 2, 3 and add each of these rhythms on the Snare Drum:

STEP 6 · Continue steps 1, 2, 3 and play this 6-bar exercise on the Snare Drum:

LESSON 2.17

STEP 1 · Start by playing either of these ostinatos on the Hi-Hat Foot:

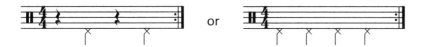

STEP 2 · Continue step 1 and add one of these ostinatos on the Bass Drum:

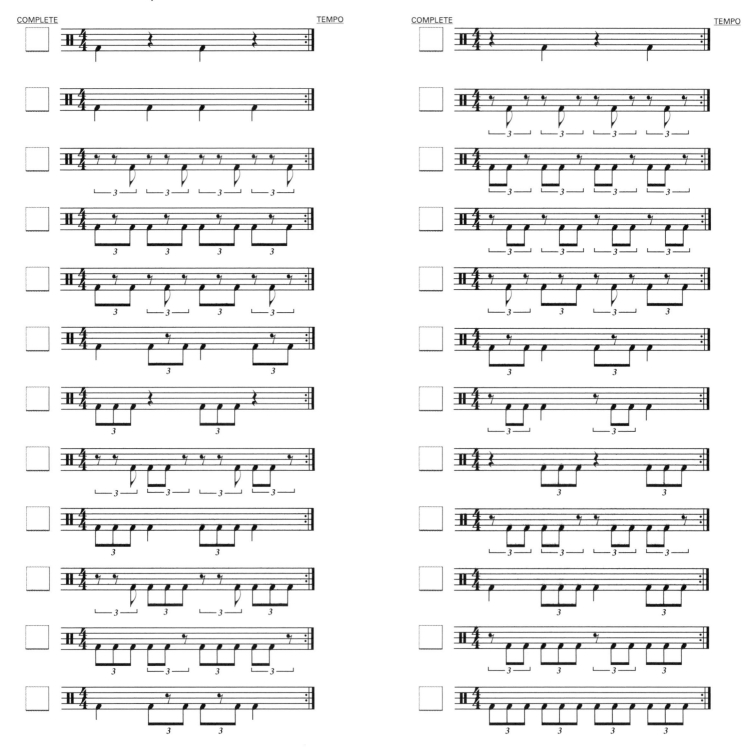

STEP 3 · Continue steps 1, 2 and add this ostinato on the Ride Cymbal:

STEP 4 · Continue steps 1, 2, 3 and add each of these rhythms on the Snare Drum:

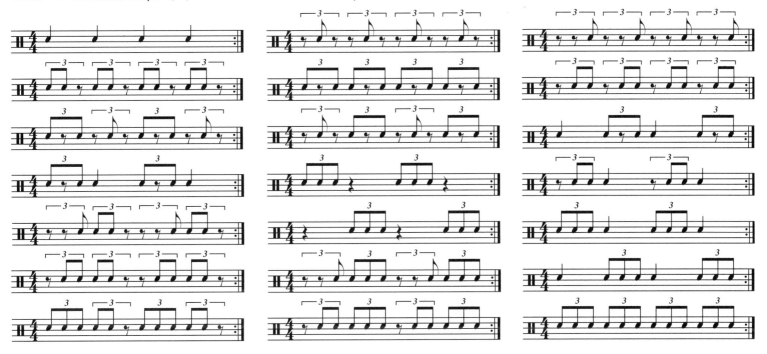

STEP 5 · Continue steps 1, 2, 3 and add each of these rhythms on the Snare Drum:

STEP 6 · Continue steps 1, 2, 3 and play this 6-bar exercise on the Snare Drum:

LESSON 2.18

STEP 1 · Start by playing either of these ostinatos on the Hi-Hat Foot:

STEP 2 · Continue step 1 and add one of these ostinatos on the Bass Drum:

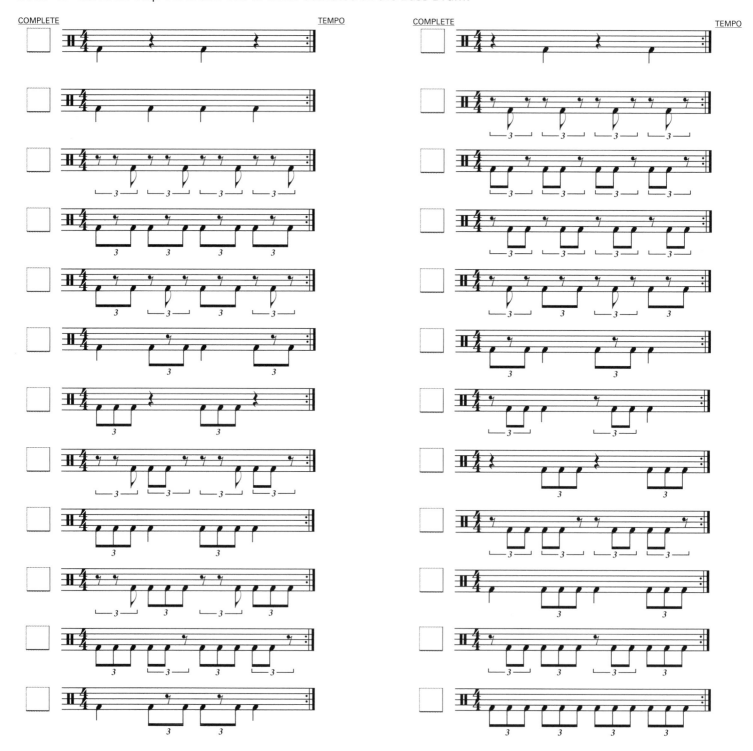

STEP 3 · Continue steps 1, 2 and add this ostinato on the Ride Cymbal:

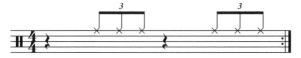

STEP 4 · Continue steps 1, 2, 3 and add each of these rhythms on the Snare Drum:

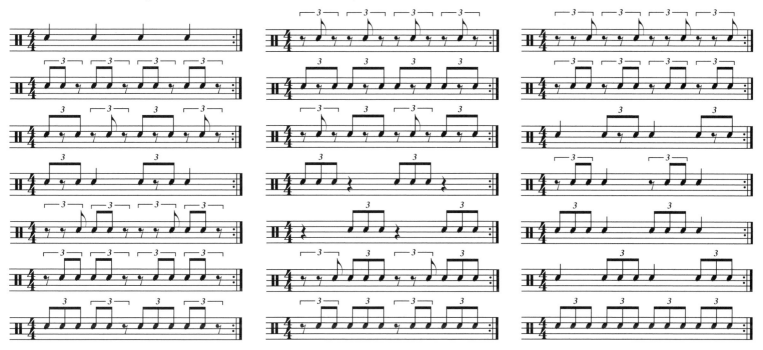

STEP 5 · Continue steps 1, 2, 3 and add each of these rhythms on the Snare Drum:

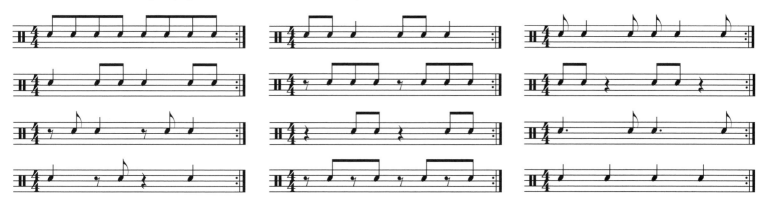

STEP 6 · Continue steps 1, 2, 3 and play this 6-bar exercise on the Snare Drum:

LESSON 2.19

STEP 1 · Start by playing either of these ostinatos on the Hi-Hat Foot:

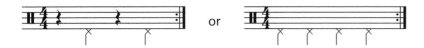

STEP 2 · Continue step 1 and add one of these ostinatos on the Bass Drum:

88

STEP 3 · Continue steps 1, 2 and add this ostinato on the Ride Cymbal:

STEP 4 · Continue steps 1, 2, 3 and add each of these rhythms on the Snare Drum:

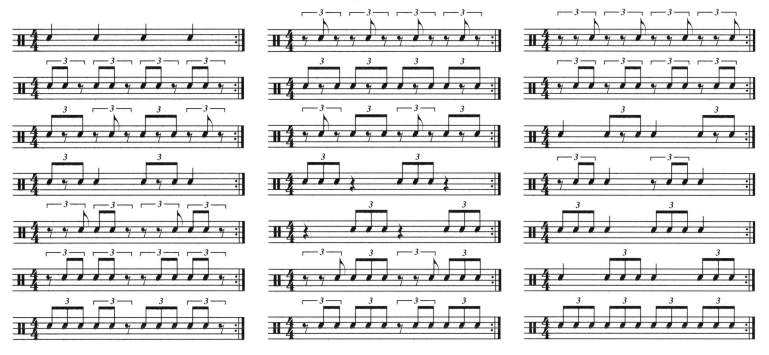

STEP 5 · Continue steps 1, 2, 3 and add each of these rhythms on the Snare Drum:

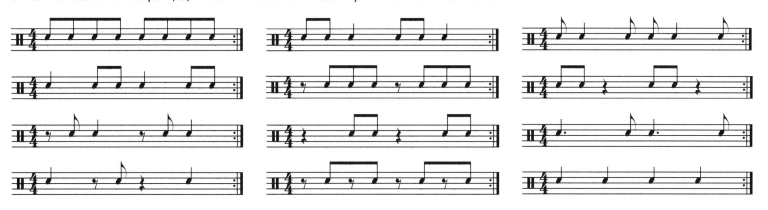

STEP 6 · Continue steps 1, 2, 3 and play this 6-bar exercise on the Snare Drum:

LESSON 2.20

STEP 1 · Start by playing either of these ostinatos on the Hi-Hat Foot:

STEP 2 · Continue step 1 and add one of these ostinatos on the Bass Drum:

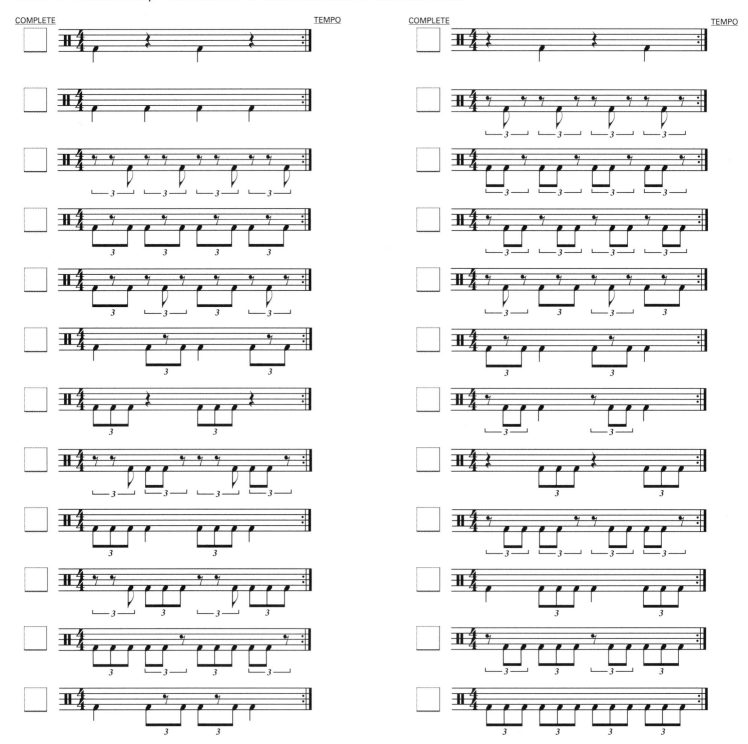

STEP 3 · Continue steps 1, 2 and add this ostinato on the Ride Cymbal:

STEP 4 · Continue steps 1, 2, 3 and add each of these rhythms on the Snare Drum:

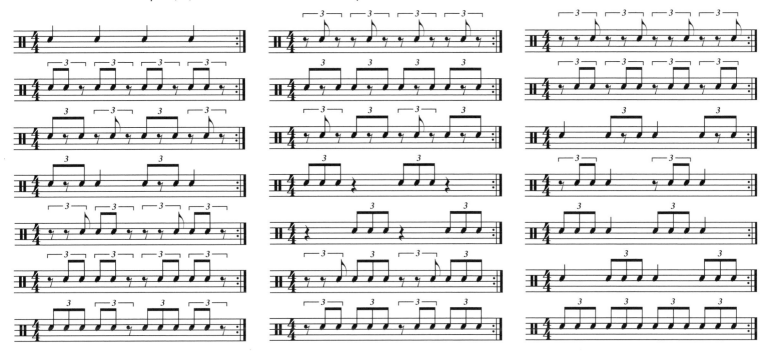

STEP 5 · Continue steps 1, 2, 3 and add each of these rhythms on the Snare Drum:

STEP 6 · Continue steps 1, 2, 3 and play this 6-bar exercise on the Snare Drum:

LESSON 2.21

STEP 1 · Start by playing either of these ostinatos on the Hi-Hat Foot:

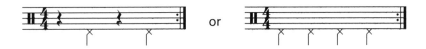

STEP 2 · Continue step 1 and add one of these ostinatos on the Bass Drum:

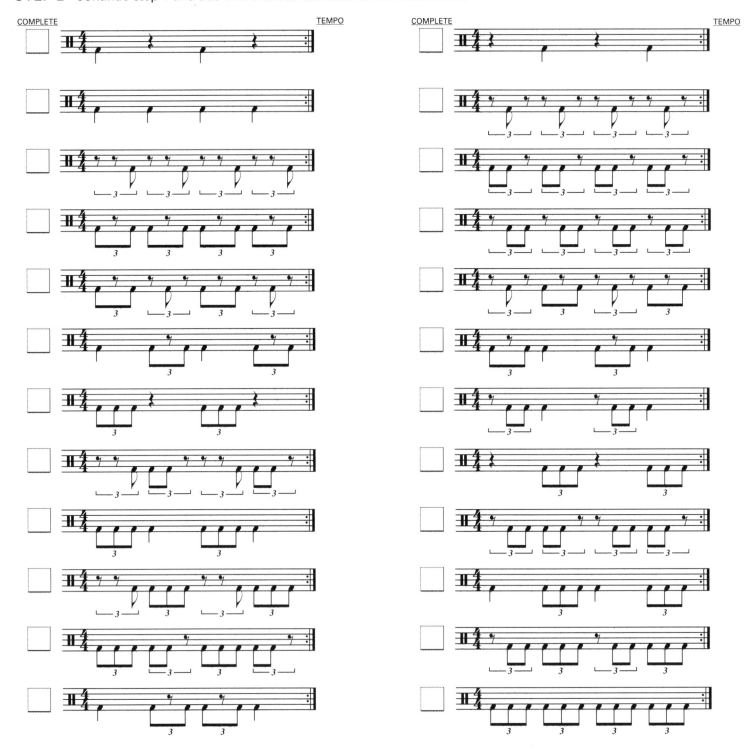

STEP 3 · Continue steps 1, 2 and add this ostinato on the Ride Cymbal:

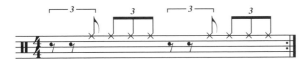

STEP 4 · Continue steps 1, 2, 3 and add each of these rhythms on the Snare Drum:

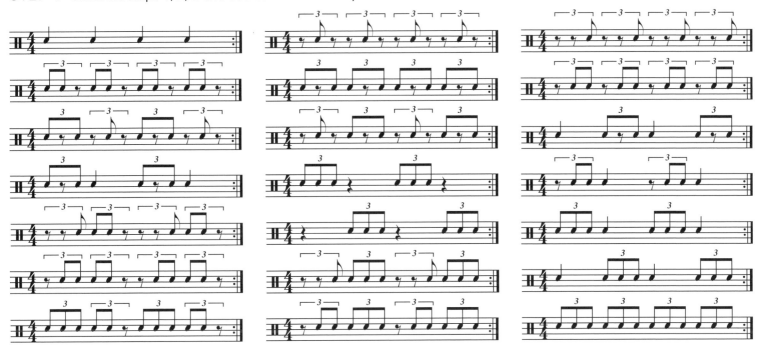

STEP 5 · Continue steps 1, 2, 3 and add each of these rhythms on the Snare Drum:

STEP 6 · Continue steps 1, 2, 3 and play this 6-bar exercise on the Snare Drum:

LESSON 2.22

STEP 1 · Start by playing either of these ostinatos on the Hi-Hat Foot:

STEP 2 · Continue step 1 and add one of these ostinatos on the Bass Drum:

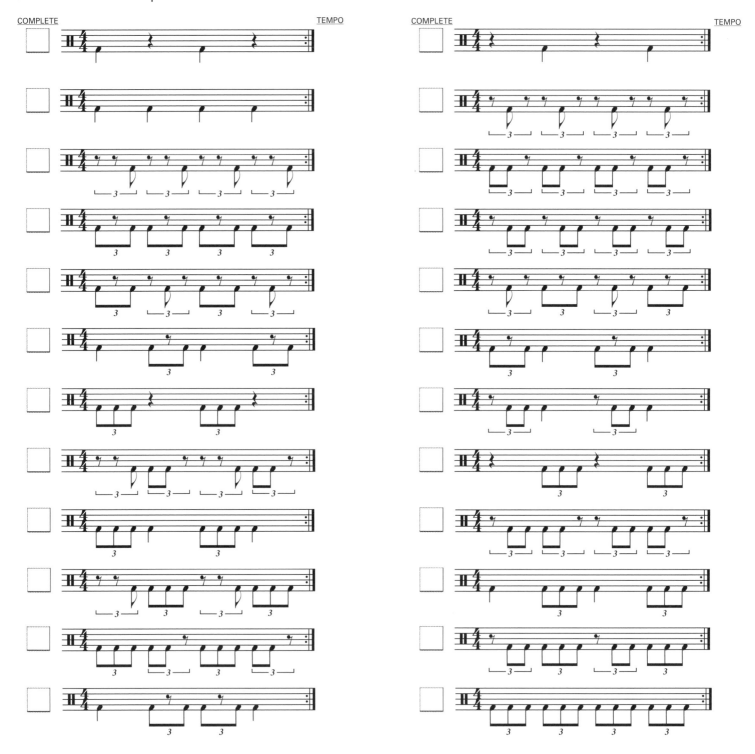

STEP 3 · Continue steps 1, 2 and add this ostinato on the Ride Cymbal:

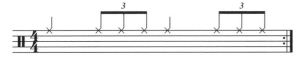

STEP 4 · Continue steps 1, 2, 3 and add each of these rhythms on the Snare Drum:

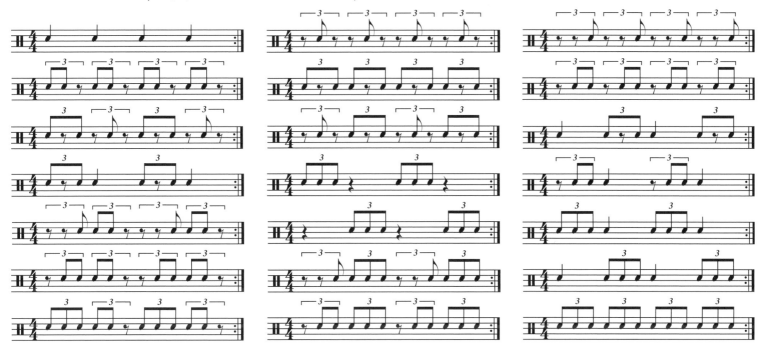

STEP 5 · Continue steps 1, 2, 3 and add each of these rhythms on the Snare Drum:

STEP 6 · Continue steps 1, 2, 3 and play this 6-bar exercise on the Snare Drum:

LESSON 2.23

STEP 1 · Start by playing either of these ostinatos on the Hi-Hat Foot:

STEP 2 · Continue step 1 and add one of these ostinatos on the Bass Drum:

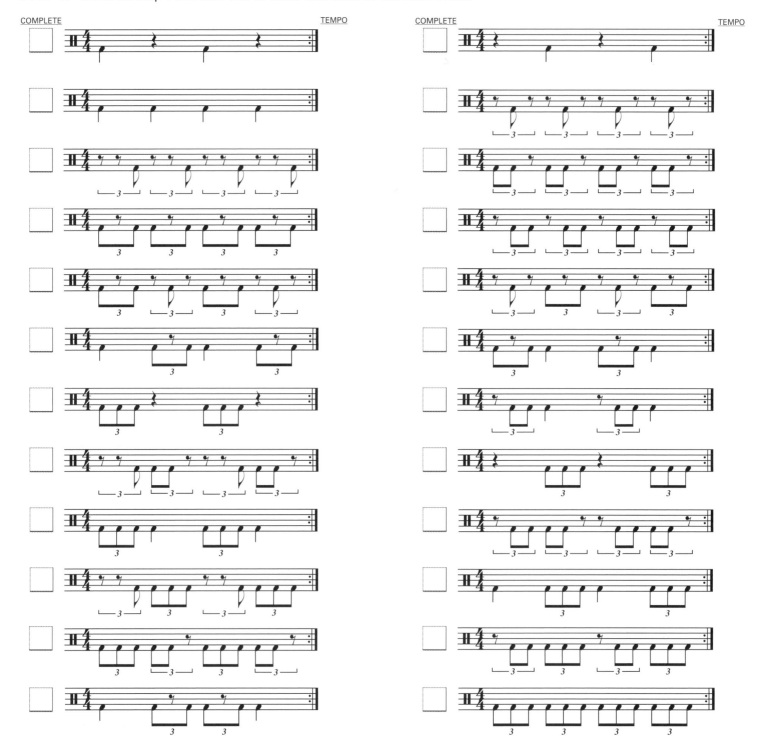

STEP 3 · Continue steps 1, 2 and add this ostinato on the Ride Cymbal:

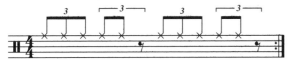

STEP 4 · Continue steps 1, 2, 3 and add each of these rhythms on the Snare Drum:

STEP 5 · Continue steps 1, 2, 3 and add each of these rhythms on the Snare Drum:

STEP 6 · Continue steps 1, 2, 3 and play this 6-bar exercise on the Snare Drum:

LESSON 2.24

STEP 1 · Start by playing either of these ostinatos on the Hi-Hat Foot:

STEP 2 · Continue step 1 and add one of these ostinatos on the Bass Drum:

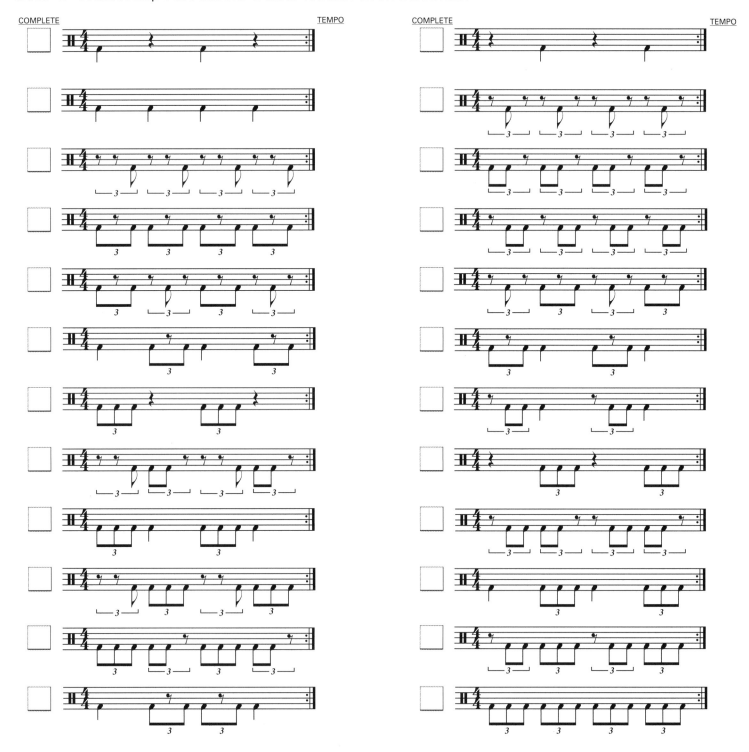

STEP 3 · Continue steps 1, 2 and add this ostinato on the Ride Cymbal:

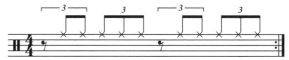

STEP 4 · Continue steps 1, 2, 3 and add each of these rhythms on the Snare Drum:

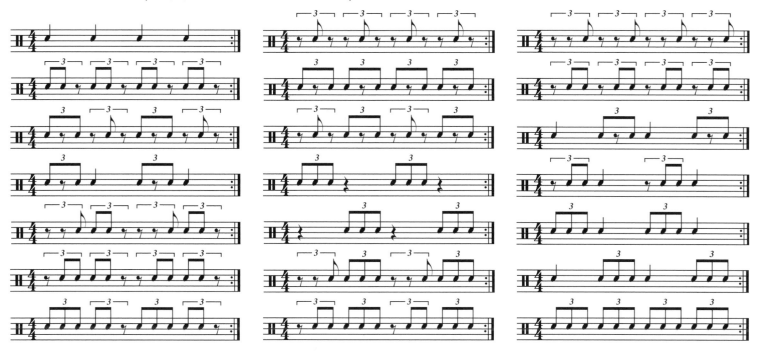

STEP 5 · Continue steps 1, 2, 3 and add each of these rhythms on the Snare Drum:

STEP 6 · Continue steps 1, 2, 3 and play this 6-bar exercise on the Snare Drum:

HI-HAT FOOT & VOCAL RHYTHMS

Additional Ostinatos for Use with Section Two

Pick a lesson you've completed and replace Step 1 with one of these Hi-Hat Foot rhythms. Play through the lesson as written, including multiple variations of Step 2. When complete, pick another Hi-Hat Foot ostinato to try. Focus on balance and take it slowly as these can be quite challenging.

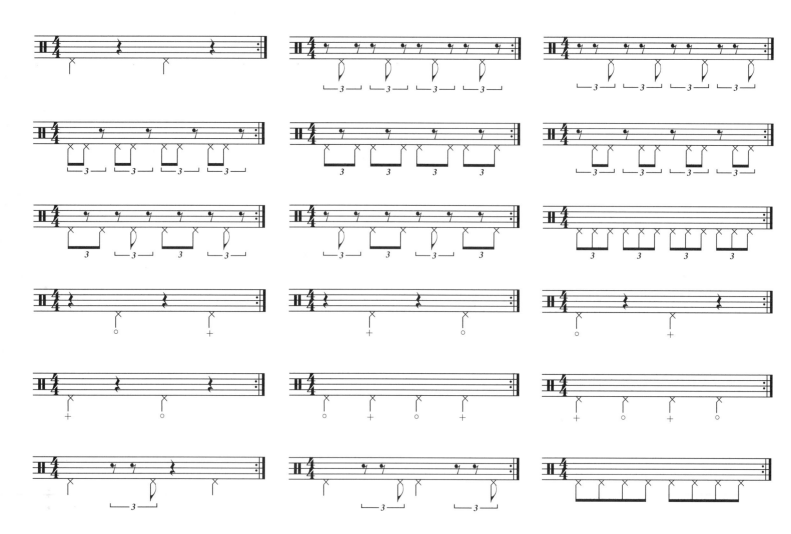

Pick a lesson you've completed and count one of these Vocal rhythms out loud. Play through the lesson as written, including multiple variations of Step 2. When complete, pick another Vocal ostinato to try. Keep your voice even and focus to make it rhythmically independent from your hands and feet.

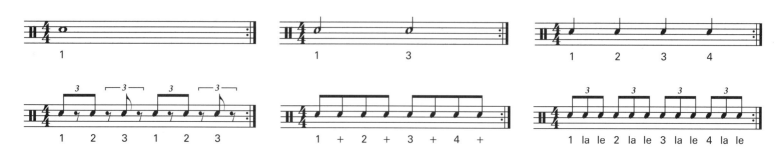

SECTION THREE
AFRO/CUBAN • LATIN

LESSON 3.1

STEP 1 · Start by playing either of these ostinatos on the Hi-Hat Foot:

STEP 2 · Continue step 1 and add one of these ostinatos on the Bass Drum:

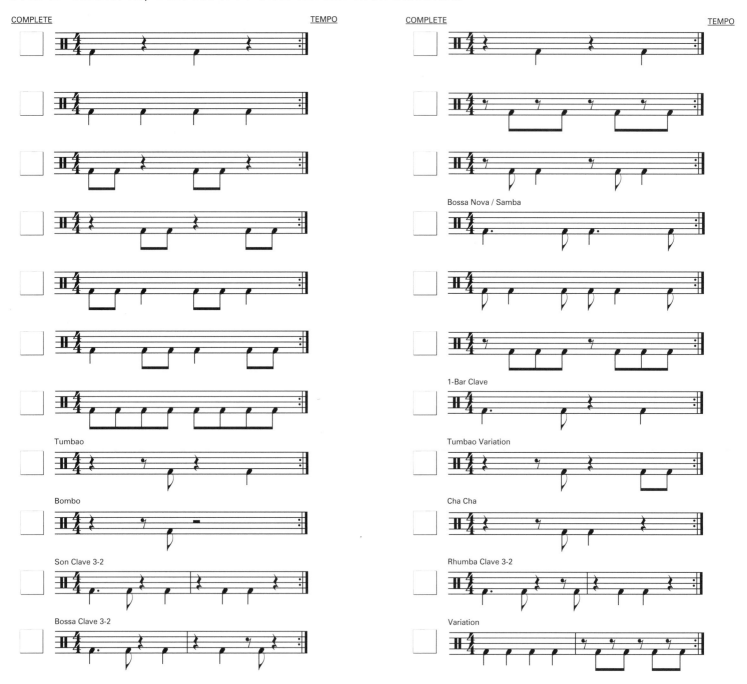

STEP 3 · Continue steps 1, 2 and add this ostinato on the Ride Cymbal:

STEP 4 · Continue steps 1, 2, 3 and add each of these rhythms on the Snare Drum:

STEP 5 · Continue steps 1, 2, 3 and add each of these rhythms on the Snare Drum and Toms:

STEP 6 · Continue steps 1, 2, 3 and play this 8-bar exercise on the Snare Drum and Toms:

LESSON 3.2

STEP 1 · Start by playing either of these ostinatos on the Hi-Hat Foot:

STEP 2 · Continue step 1 and add one of these ostinatos on the Bass Drum:

STEP 3 · Continue steps 1, 2 and add this ostinato on the Ride Cymbal:

STEP 4 · Continue steps 1, 2, 3 and add each of these rhythms on the Snare Drum:

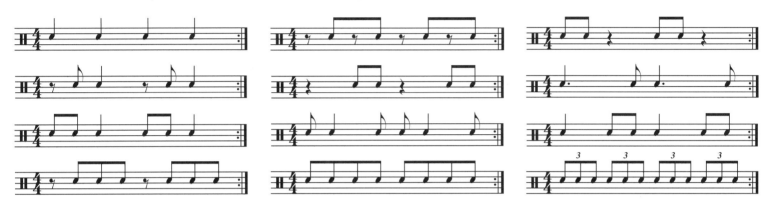

STEP 5 · Continue steps 1, 2, 3 and add each of these rhythms on the Snare Drum and Toms:

STEP 6 · Continue steps 1, 2, 3 and play this 8-bar exercise on the Snare Drum and Toms:

LESSON 3.3

STEP 1 · Start by playing either of these ostinatos on the Hi-Hat Foot:

or

STEP 2 · Continue step 1 and add one of these ostinatos on the Bass Drum:

STEP 3 · Continue steps 1, 2 and add this ostinato on the Ride Cymbal:

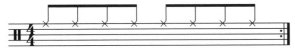

STEP 4 · Continue steps 1, 2, 3 and add each of these rhythms on the Snare Drum:

STEP 5 · Continue steps 1, 2, 3 and add each of these rhythms on the Snare Drum and Toms:

STEP 6 · Continue steps 1, 2, 3 and play this 8-bar exercise on the Snare Drum and Toms:

LESSON 3.4

STEP 1 · Start by playing either of these ostinatos on the Hi-Hat Foot:

STEP 2 · Continue step 1 and add one of these ostinatos on the Bass Drum:

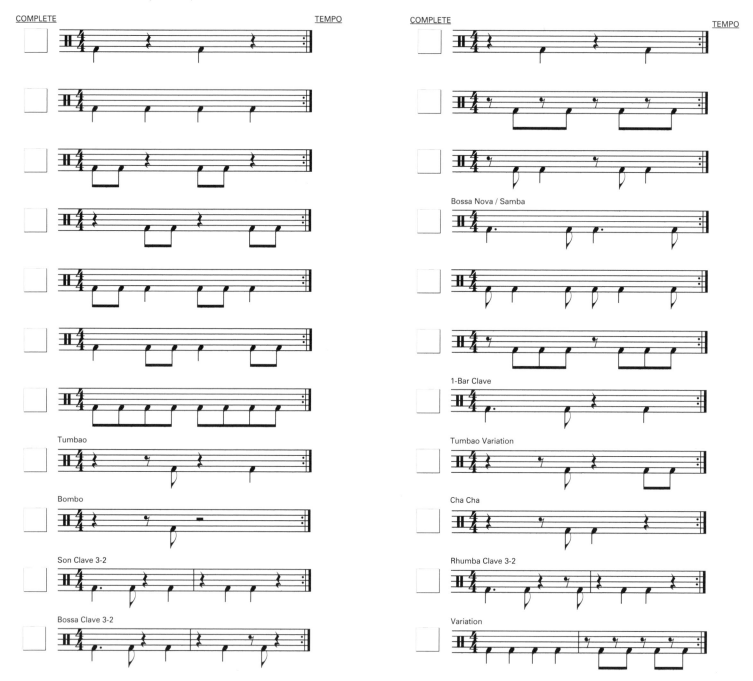

STEP 3 · Continue steps 1, 2 and add this ostinato on the Ride Cymbal:

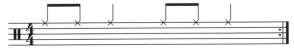

STEP 4 · Continue steps 1, 2, 3 and add each of these rhythms on the Snare Drum:

STEP 5 · Continue steps 1, 2, 3 and add each of these rhythms on the Snare Drum and Toms:

STEP 6 · Continue steps 1, 2, 3 and play this 8-bar exercise on the Snare Drum and Toms:

LESSON 3.5

STEP 1 · Start by playing either of these ostinatos on the Hi-Hat Foot:

STEP 2 · Continue step 1 and add one of these ostinatos on the Bass Drum:

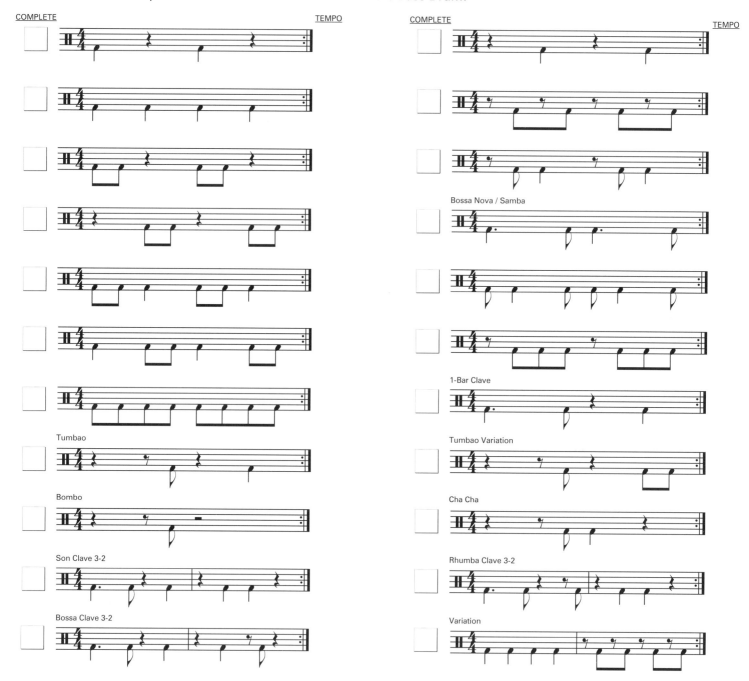

STEP 3 · Continue steps 1, 2 and add this ostinato on the Ride Cymbal:

STEP 4 · Continue steps 1, 2, 3 and add each of these rhythms on the Snare Drum:

STEP 5 · Continue steps 1, 2, 3 and add each of these rhythms on the Snare Drum and Toms:

STEP 6 · Continue steps 1, 2, 3 and play this 8-bar exercise on the Snare Drum and Toms:

LESSON 3.6

STEP 1 · Start by playing either of these ostinatos on the Hi-Hat Foot:

STEP 2 · Continue step 1 and add one of these ostinatos on the Bass Drum:

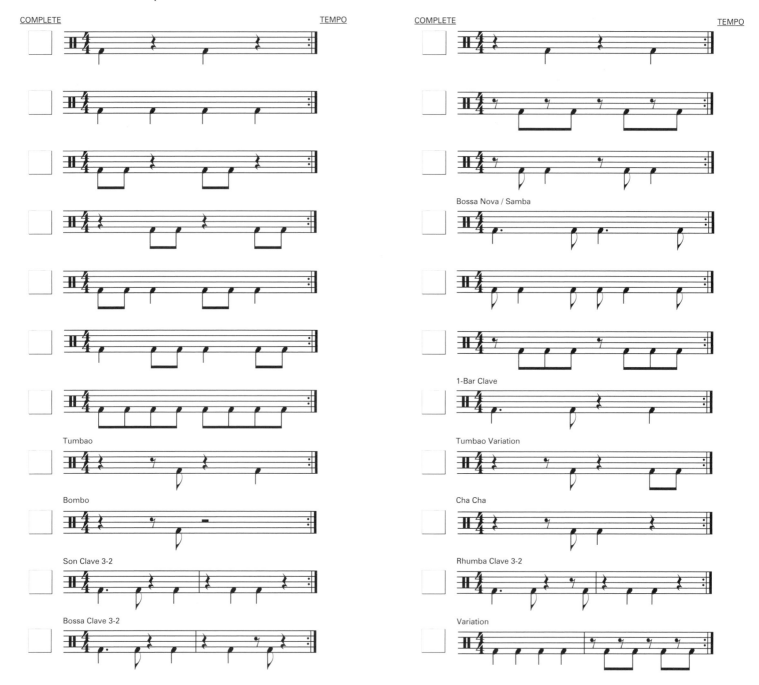

STEP 3 · Continue steps 1, 2 and add this ostinato on the Ride Cymbal:

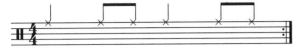

STEP 4 · Continue steps 1, 2, 3 and add each of these rhythms on the Snare Drum:

STEP 5 · Continue steps 1, 2, 3 and add each of these rhythms on the Snare Drum and Toms:

STEP 6 · Continue steps 1, 2, 3 and play this 8-bar exercise on the Snare Drum and Toms:

LESSON 3.7

STEP 1 · Start by playing either of these ostinatos on the Hi-Hat Foot:

STEP 2 · Continue step 1 and add one of these ostinatos on the Bass Drum:

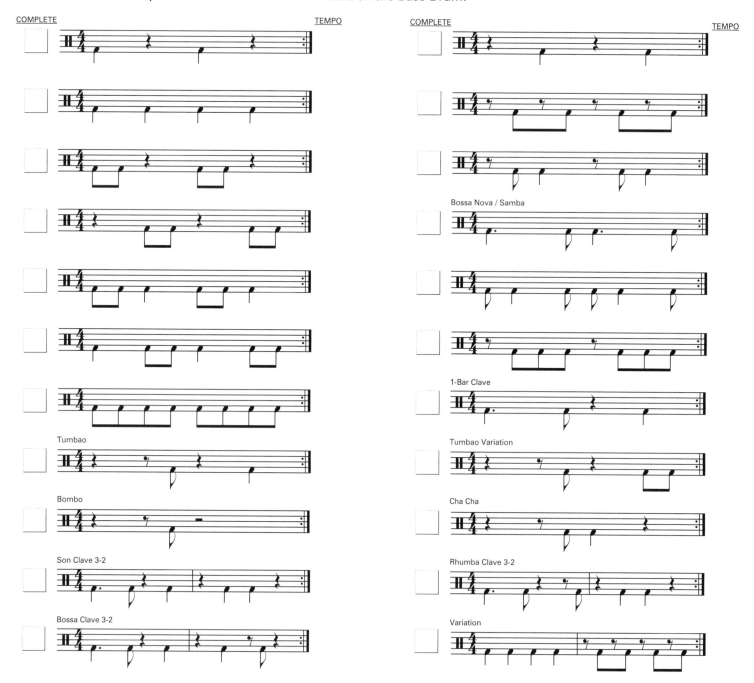

STEP 3 · Continue steps 1, 2 and add this ostinato on the Ride Cymbal:

STEP 4 · Continue steps 1, 2, 3 and add each of these rhythms on the Snare Drum:

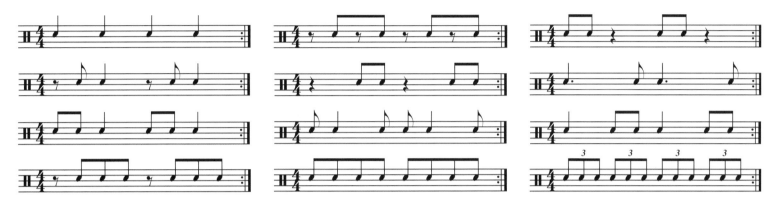

STEP 5 · Continue steps 1, 2, 3 and add each of these rhythms on the Snare Drum and Toms:

STEP 6 · Continue steps 1, 2, 3 and play this 8-bar exercise on the Snare Drum and Toms:

LESSON 3.8

STEP 1 · Start by playing either of these ostinatos on the Hi-Hat Foot:

STEP 2 · Continue step 1 and add one of these ostinatos on the Bass Drum:

STEP 3 · Continue steps 1, 2 and add this ostinato on the Ride Cymbal:

STEP 4 · Continue steps 1, 2, 3 and add each of these rhythms on the Snare Drum:

STEP 5 · Continue steps 1, 2, 3 and add each of these rhythms on the Snare Drum and Toms:

STEP 6 · Continue steps 1, 2, 3 and play this 8-bar exercise on the Snare Drum and Toms:

LESSON 3.9

STEP 1 · Start by playing either of these ostinatos on the Hi-Hat Foot:

STEP 2 · Continue step 1 and add one of these ostinatos on the Bass Drum:

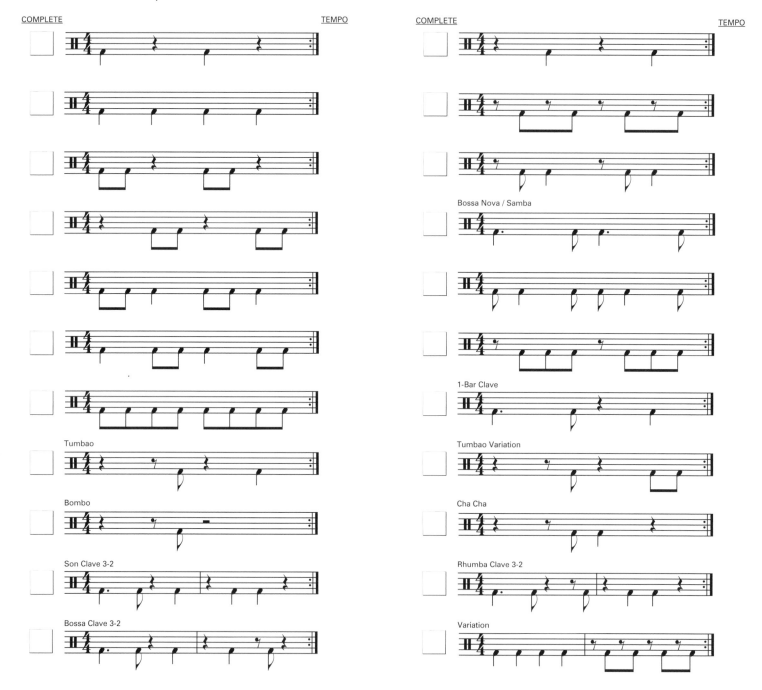

STEP 3 · Continue steps 1, 2 and add this ostinato on the Ride Cymbal:

STEP 4 · Continue steps 1, 2, 3 and add each of these rhythms on the Snare Drum:

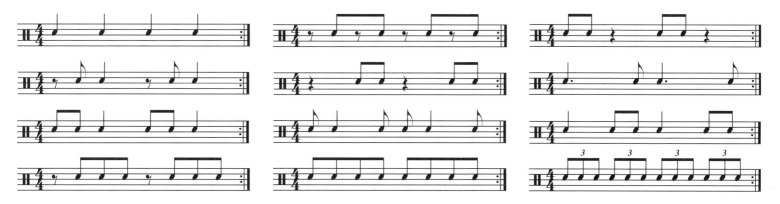

STEP 5 · Continue steps 1, 2, 3 and add each of these rhythms on the Snare Drum and Toms:

STEP 6 · Continue steps 1, 2, 3 and play this 8-bar exercise on the Snare Drum and Toms:

LESSON 3.10

STEP 1 · Start by playing either of these ostinatos on the Hi-Hat Foot:

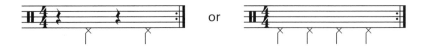

STEP 2 · Continue step 1 and add one of these ostinatos on the Bass Drum:

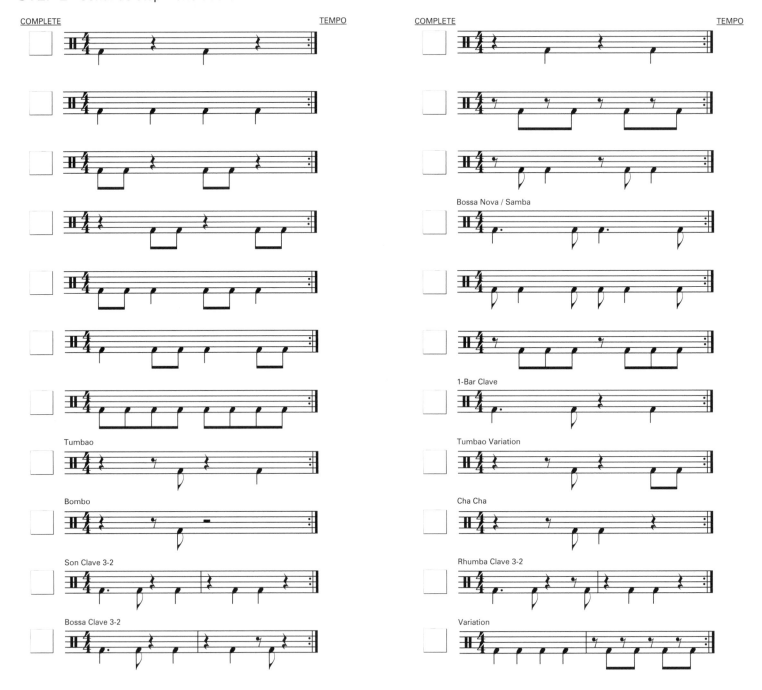

STEP 3 · Continue steps 1, 2 and add this ostinato on the Ride Cymbal:

STEP 4 · Continue steps 1, 2, 3 and add each of these rhythms on the Snare Drum:

STEP 5 · Continue steps 1, 2, 3 and add each of these rhythms on the Snare Drum and Toms:

STEP 6 · Continue steps 1, 2, 3 and play this 8-bar exercise on the Snare Drum and Toms:

LESSON 3.11

STEP 1 · Start by playing either of these ostinatos on the Hi-Hat Foot:

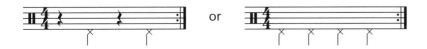

STEP 2 · Continue step 1 and add one of these ostinatos on the Bass Drum:

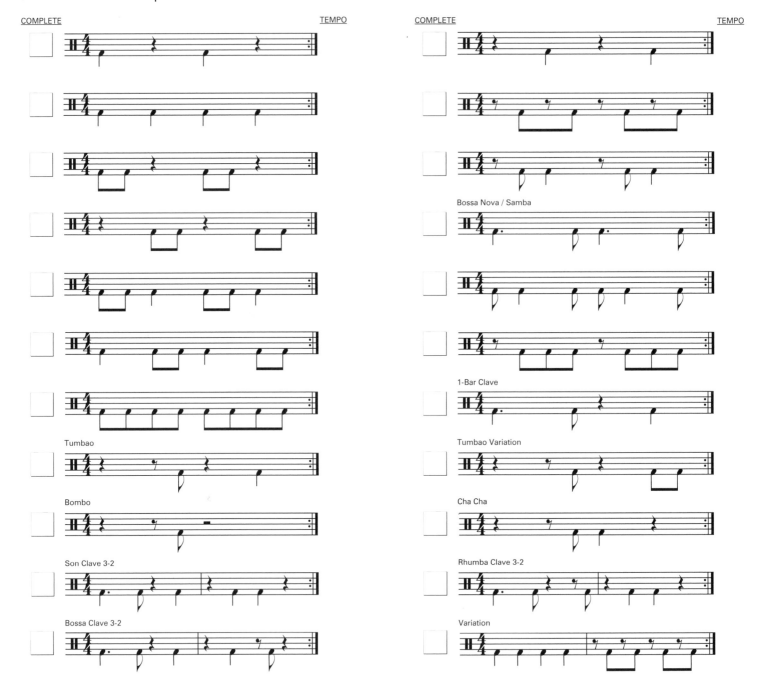

STEP 3 · Continue steps 1, 2 and add this ostinato on the Ride Cymbal:

STEP 4 · Continue steps 1, 2, 3 and add each of these rhythms on the Snare Drum:

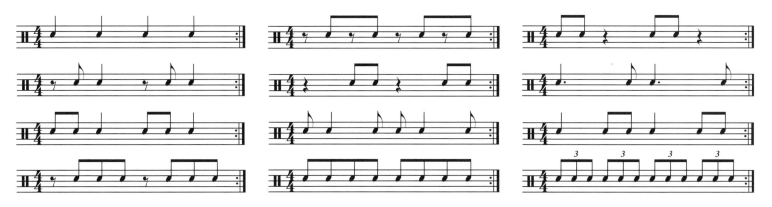

STEP 5 · Continue steps 1, 2, 3 and add each of these rhythms on the Snare Drum and Toms:

STEP 6 · Continue steps 1, 2, 3 and play this 8-bar exercise on the Snare Drum and Toms:

LESSON 3.12

STEP 1 · Start by playing either of these ostinatos on the Hi-Hat Foot:

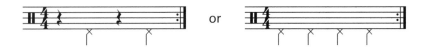

STEP 2 · Continue step 1 and add one of these ostinatos on the Bass Drum:

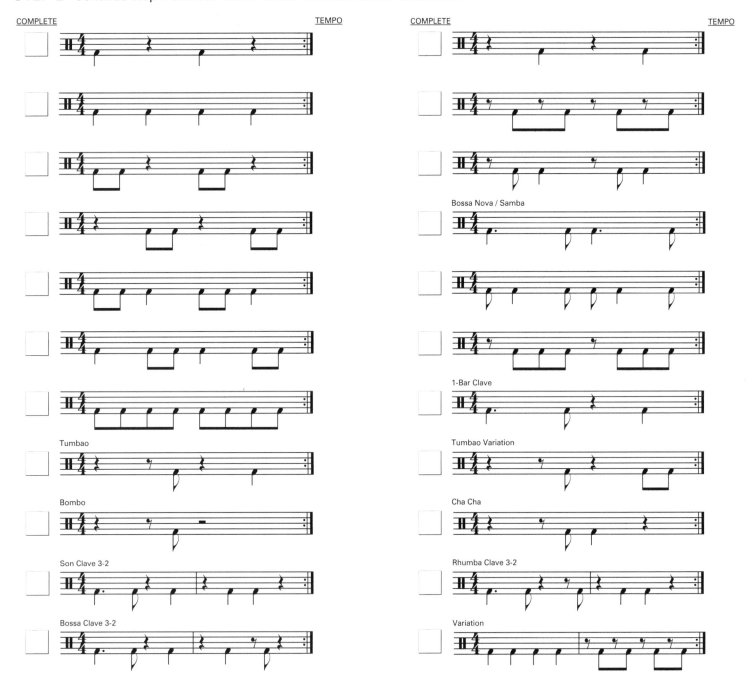

STEP 3 · Continue steps 1, 2 and add this ostinato on the Ride Cymbal:

1-Bar Clave

STEP 4 · Continue steps 1, 2, 3 and add each of these rhythms on the Snare Drum:

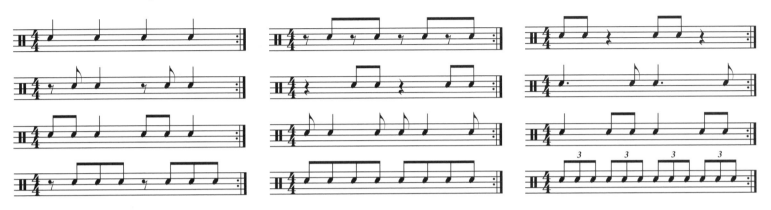

STEP 5 · Continue steps 1, 2, 3 and add each of these rhythms on the Snare Drum and Toms:

STEP 6 · Continue steps 1, 2, 3 and play this 8-bar exercise on the Snare Drum and Toms:

LESSON 3.13

STEP 1 · Start by playing either of these ostinatos on the Hi-Hat Foot:

STEP 2 · Continue step 1 and add one of these ostinatos on the Bass Drum:

STEP 3 · Continue steps 1, 2 and add this ostinato on the Ride Cymbal:

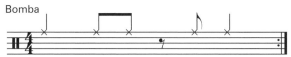

STEP 4 · Continue steps 1, 2, 3 and add each of these rhythms on the Snare Drum:

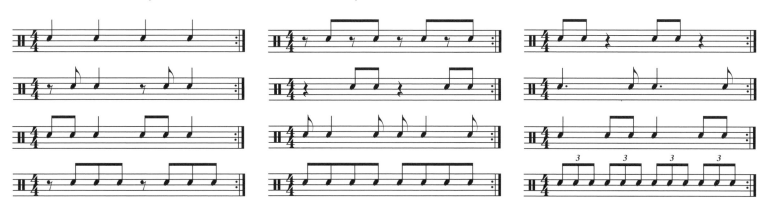

STEP 5 · Continue steps 1, 2, 3 and add each of these rhythms on the Snare Drum and Toms:

STEP 6 · Continue steps 1, 2, 3 and play this 8-bar exercise on the Snare Drum and Toms:

LESSON 3.14

STEP 1 · Start by playing either of these ostinatos on the Hi-Hat Foot:

STEP 2 · Continue step 1 and add one of these ostinatos on the Bass Drum:

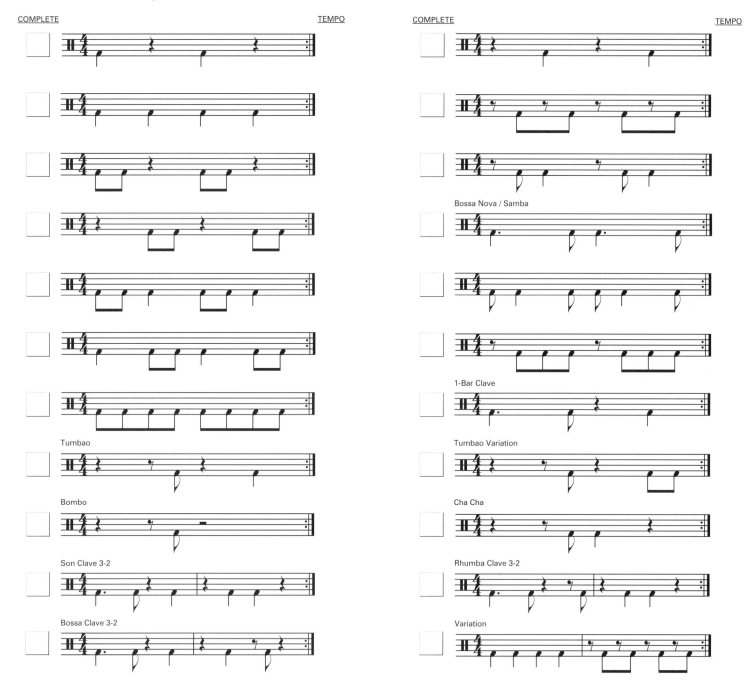

STEP 3 · Continue steps 1, 2 and add this ostinato on the Ride Cymbal:

Baiao

STEP 4 · Continue steps 1, 2, 3 and add each of these rhythms on the Snare Drum:

STEP 5 · Continue steps 1, 2, 3 and add each of these rhythms on the Snare Drum and Toms:

1-Bar Clave

Son Clave 3-2

Rhumba Clave 3-2

Bossa Clave 3-2

Guaguanco 3-2

Cha Cha

Mozambique 2-3

Songo 2-3

Bomba

Conga 2-3

Partido Alto 4-3

Rai

World Beat

Soukous

Mambo 2-3

Merengue

Pilon 2-3

Plena

STEP 6 · Continue steps 1, 2, 3 and play this 8-bar exercise on the Snare Drum and Toms:

LESSON 3.15

STEP 1 · Start by playing either of these ostinatos on the Hi-Hat Foot:

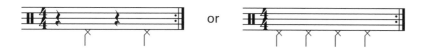

STEP 2 · Continue step 1 and add one of these ostinatos on the Bass Drum:

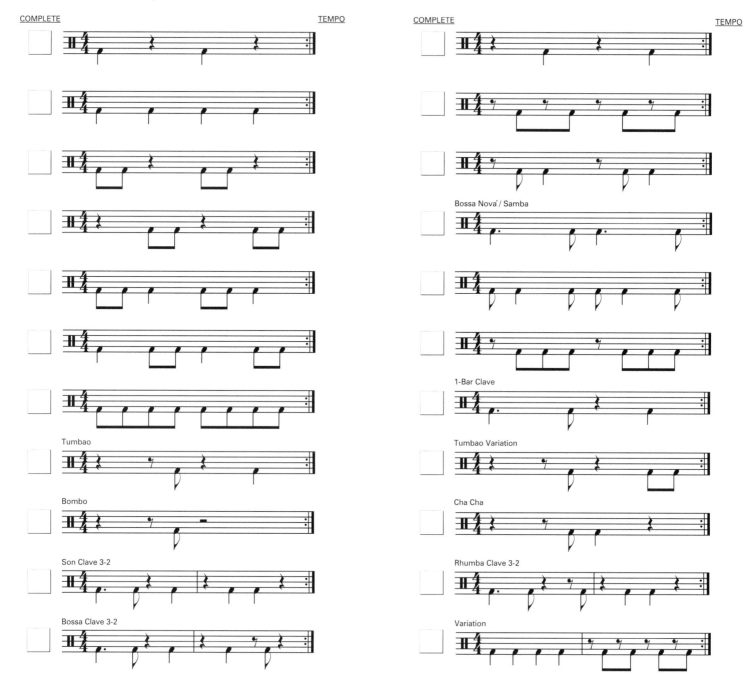

STEP 3 · Continue steps 1, 2 and add this ostinato on the Ride Cymbal:

STEP 4 · Continue steps 1, 2, 3 and add each of these rhythms on the Snare Drum:

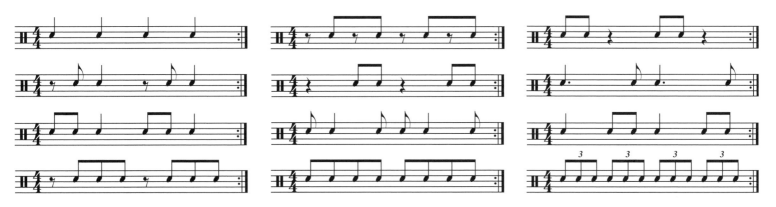

STEP 5 · Continue steps 1, 2, 3 and add each of these rhythms on the Snare Drum and Toms:

STEP 6 · Continue steps 1, 2, 3 and play this 8-bar exercise on the Snare Drum and Toms:

LESSON 3.16

STEP 1 · Start by playing either of these ostinatos on the Hi-Hat Foot:

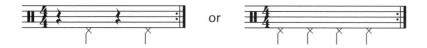

STEP 2 · Continue step 1 and add one of these ostinatos on the Bass Drum:

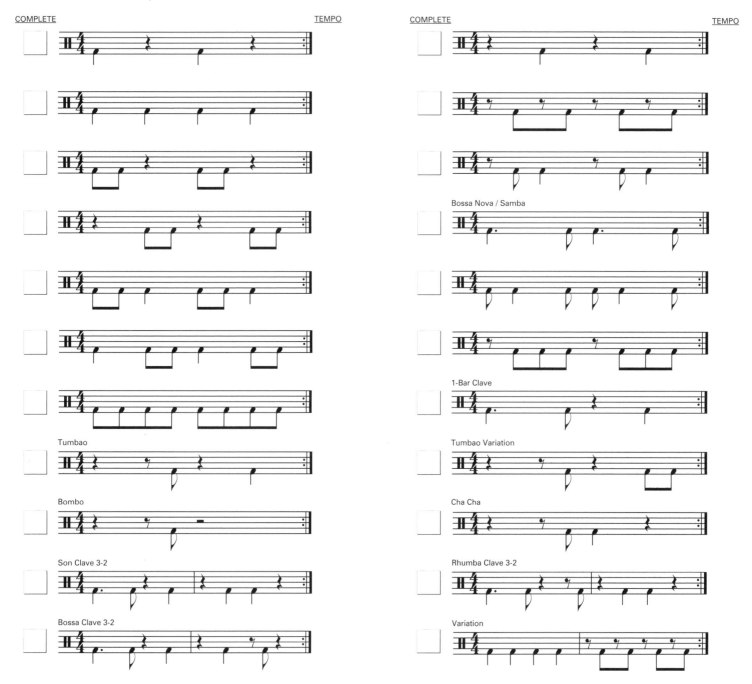

STEP 3 · Continue steps 1, 2 and add this ostinato on the Ride Cymbal:

STEP 4 · Continue steps 1, 2, 3 and add each of these rhythms on the Snare Drum:

STEP 5 · Continue steps 1, 2, 3 and add each of these rhythms on the Snare Drum and Toms:

STEP 6 · Continue steps 1, 2, 3 and play this 8-bar exercise on the Snare Drum and Toms:

LESSON 3.17

STEP 1 · Start by playing either of these ostinatos on the Hi-Hat Foot:

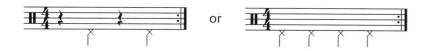

STEP 2 · Continue step 1 and add one of these ostinatos on the Bass Drum:

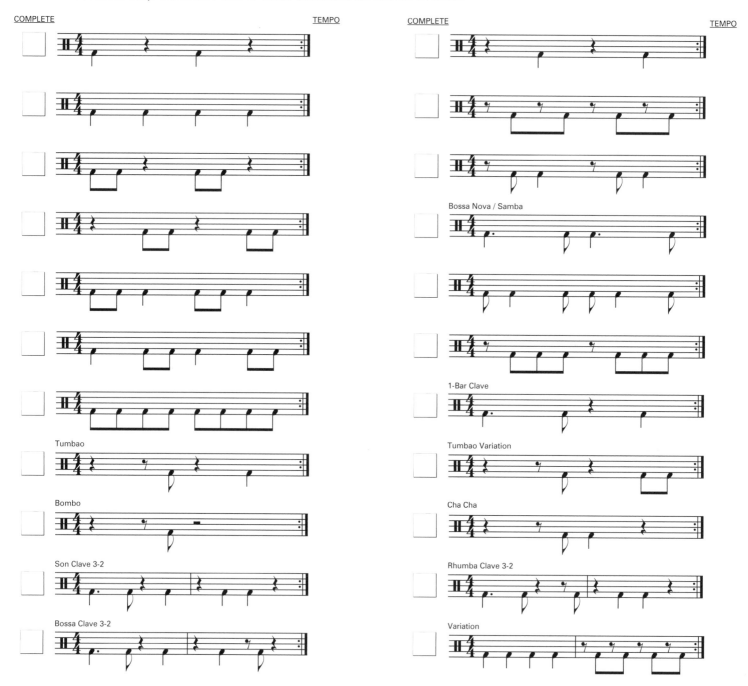

STEP 3 · Continue steps 1, 2 and add this ostinato on the Ride Cymbal:

STEP 4 · Continue steps 1, 2, 3 and add each of these rhythms on the Snare Drum:

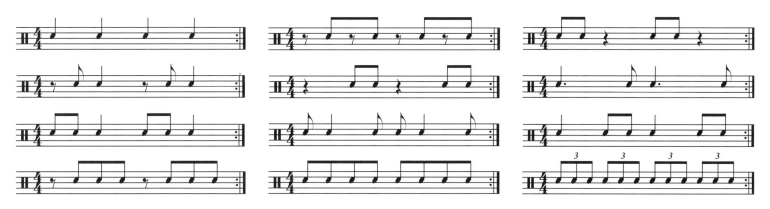

STEP 5 · Continue steps 1, 2, 3 and add each of these rhythms on the Snare Drum and Toms:

STEP 6 · Continue steps 1, 2, 3 and play this 8-bar exercise on the Snare Drum and Toms:

LESSON 3.18

STEP 1 · Start by playing either of these ostinatos on the Hi-Hat Foot:

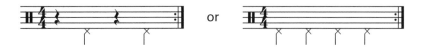

STEP 2 · Continue step 1 and add one of these ostinatos on the Bass Drum:

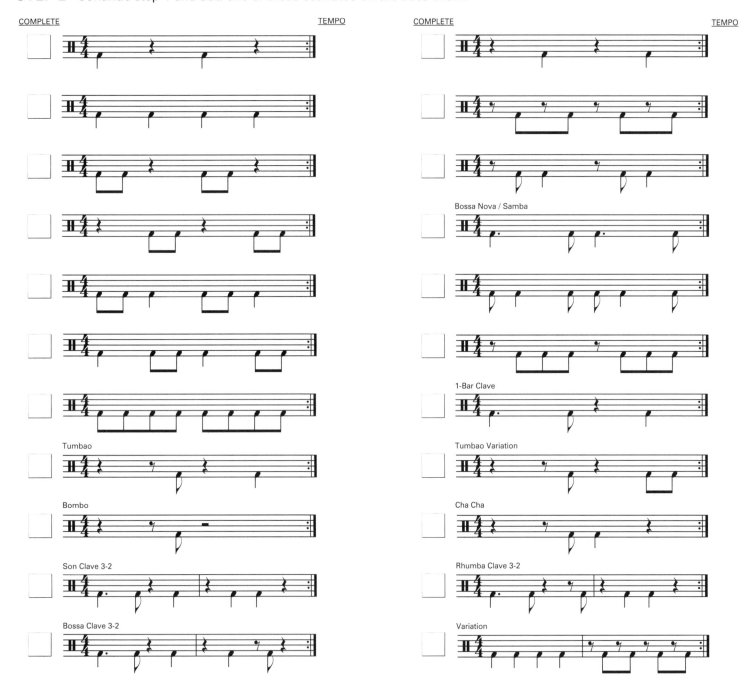

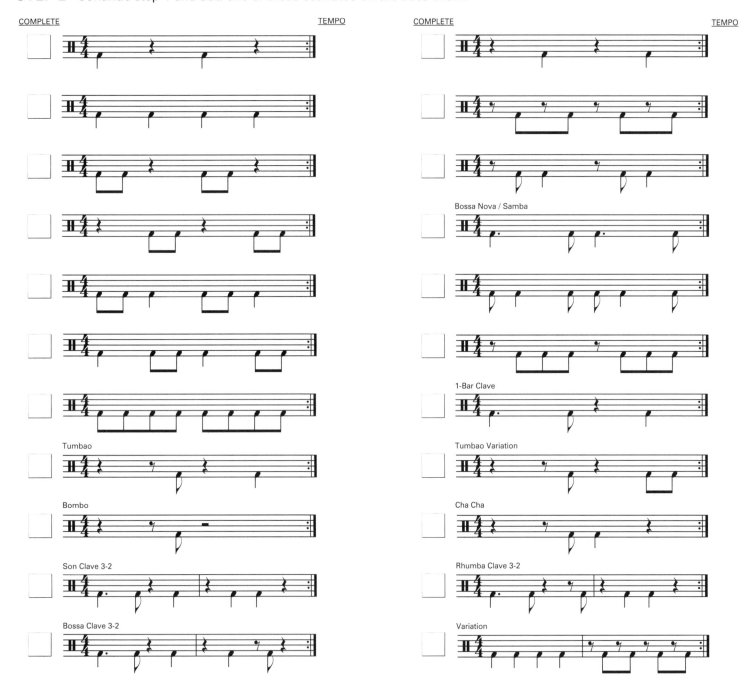

STEP 3 · Continue steps 1, 2 and add this ostinato on the Ride Cymbal:

STEP 4 · Continue steps 1, 2, 3 and add each of these rhythms on the Snare Drum:

STEP 5 · Continue steps 1, 2, 3 and add each of these rhythms on the Snare Drum and Toms:

STEP 6 · Continue steps 1, 2, 3 and play this 8-bar exercise on the Snare Drum and Toms:

LESSON 3.19

STEP 1 · Start by playing either of these ostinatos on the Hi-Hat Foot:

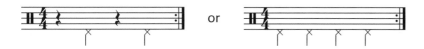

STEP 2 · Continue step 1 and add one of these ostinatos on the Bass Drum:

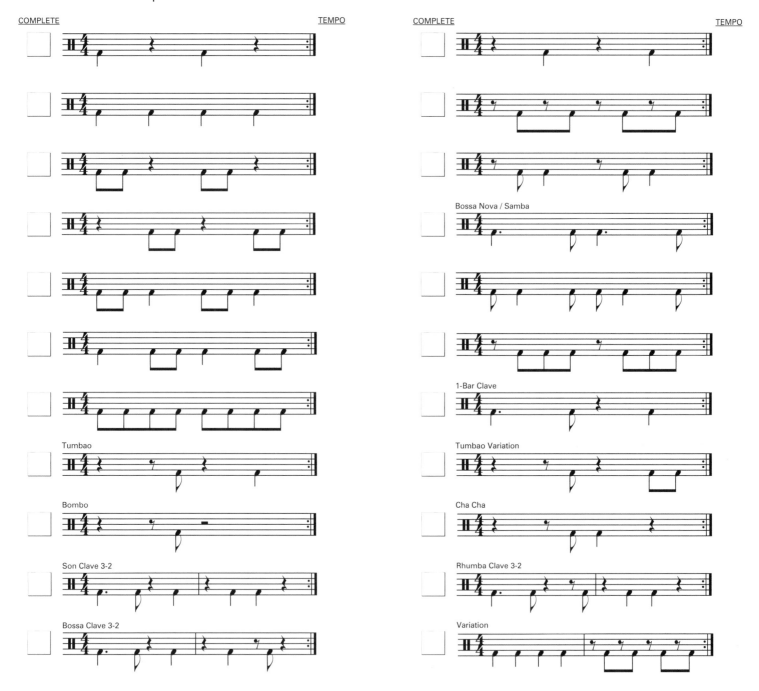

STEP 3 · Continue steps 1, 2 and add this ostinato on the Ride Cymbal:

STEP 4 · Continue steps 1, 2, 3 and add each of these rhythms on the Snare Drum:

STEP 5 · Continue steps 1, 2, 3 and add each of these rhythms on the Snare Drum and Toms:

STEP 6 · Continue steps 1, 2, 3 and play this 8-bar exercise on the Snare Drum and Toms:

LESSON 3.20

STEP 1 · Start by playing either of these ostinatos on the Hi-Hat Foot:

STEP 2 · Continue step 1 and add one of these ostinatos on the Bass Drum:

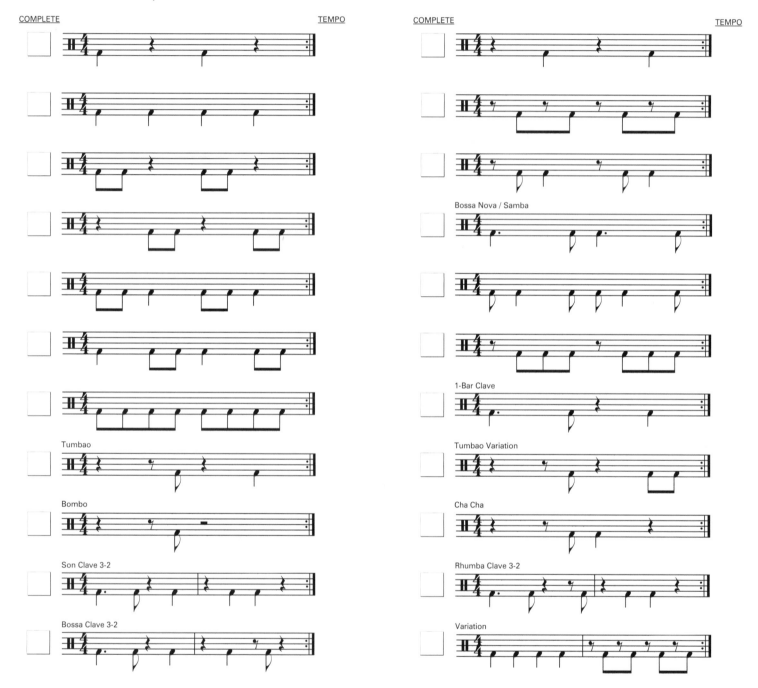

STEP 3 · Continue steps 1, 2 and add this ostinato on the Ride Cymbal:

STEP 4 · Continue steps 1, 2, 3 and add each of these rhythms on the Snare Drum:

STEP 5 · Continue steps 1, 2, 3 and add each of these rhythms on the Snare Drum and Toms:

STEP 6 · Continue steps 1, 2, 3 and play this 8-bar exercise on the Snare Drum and Toms:

HI-HAT FOOT & VOCAL RHYTHMS

Additional Ostinatos for Use with Section Three

Pick a lesson you've completed and replace Step 1 with one of these Hi-Hat Foot rhythms. Play through the lesson as written, including multiple variations of Step 2. When complete, pick another Hi-Hat Foot ostinato to try. Focus on balance and take it slowly as these can be quite challenging.

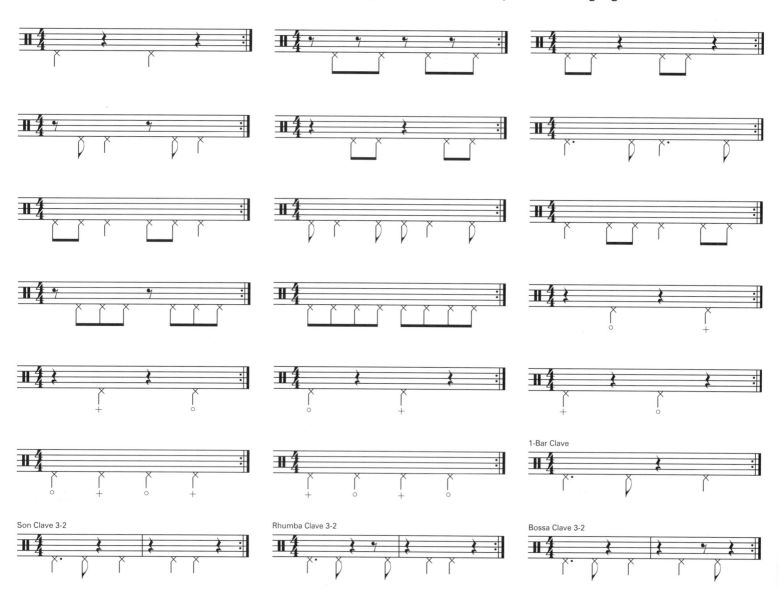

Pick a lesson you've completed and count one of these Vocal rhythms out loud. Play through the lesson as written, including multiple variations of Step 2. When complete, pick another Vocal ostinato to try. Keep your voice even and focus to make it rhythmically independent from your hands and feet.

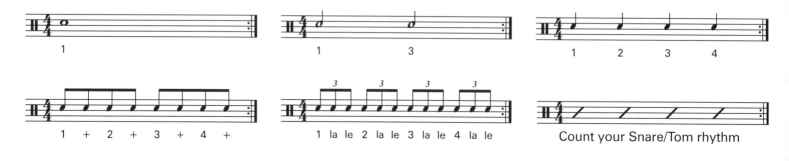

READING

The following pages contain 32-bar melodies that combine the rhythms you have learned in the previous sections. Use these variations with any lesson already practiced to strengthen and build upon what you have learned.

1. Pick a lesson to be played again. This time, substitute one of the reading texts for steps 4, 5, and 6. You can play the reading texts in the following ways:
   - on the snare drum as written;
   - on the snare drum with short notes (eighth, eighth triplet, sixteenth) played quietly, and long notes (whole, half, quarter) played loudly;
   - with short notes (eighth, eighth triplet, sixteenth) played on the snare, and long notes (whole, half, quarter) played on the high, medium, or low tom;
   - on the snare with short notes (eighth, eighth triplet, sixteenth) played as written, and long notes (whole, half, quarter) played as buzz strokes;
   - on the snare with short notes (eighth, eighth triplet, sixteenth) played as written, and long notes (whole, half, quarter) played as double strokes.

2. Pick a lesson to be played again. This time, substitute one of the reading texts for steps 2, 4, 5, and 6. You can play the reading texts in the following ways:
   - on the bass drum as written;
   - with short notes (eighth, eighth triplet, sixteenth) played on the snare, and long notes (whole, half, quarter) played on the bass drum;
   - with short notes (eighth, eighth triplet, sixteenth) played on the snare as buzz strokes, and long notes (whole, half, quarter) played on the bass drum;
   - with short notes (eighth, eighth triplet, sixteenth) played on the snare as double strokes, and long notes (whole, half, quarter) played on the bass drum.

3. Create your own interesting new ways to read the music!

READING A

READING B

READING C

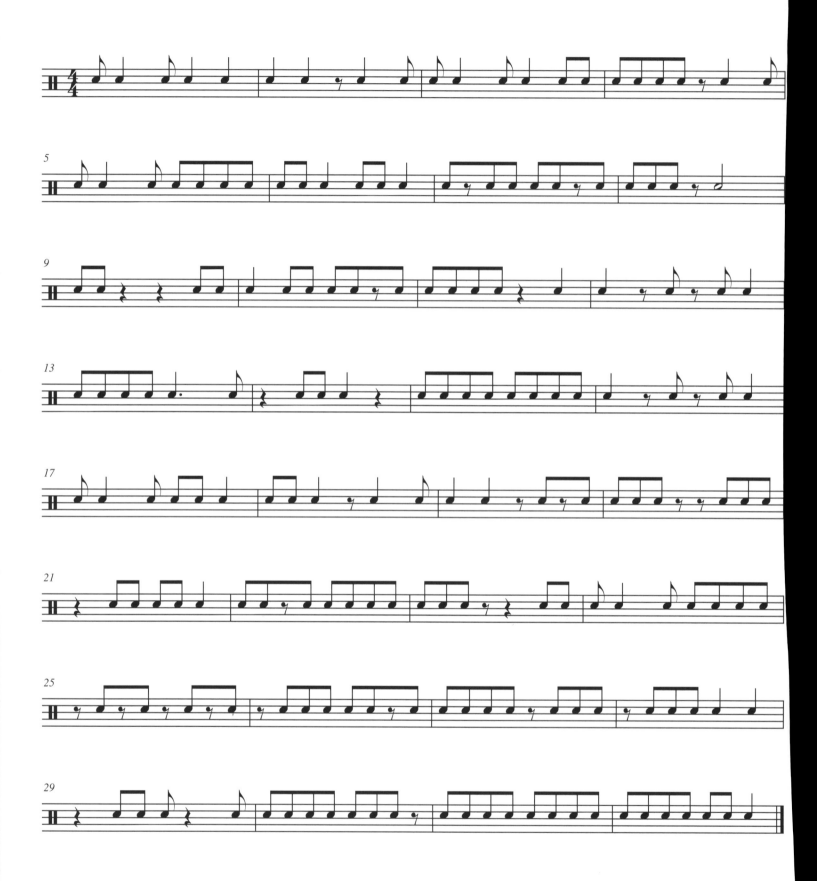

READING D

READING E

READING F

READING G

READING H

READING I

READING J

ABOUT THE AUTHOR

Blake Paulson (born April 10, 1978) is an American drummer residing in Los Angeles, CA. An active touring and session drummer, he has worked for many talented independent and major label artists including Miley Cyrus, Demi Lovato, the Jonas Brothers, and Hoku. He is also a founding member and business director of LA's team of session musicians, The Backliners.

Blake's education includes a Bachelor of Arts from Berklee College of Music in Boston, MA. In 2000 he was awarded the school's Professional Music Achievement Award. Blake's training comes from some of the finest drummers in America: Scott Crosbie, Paul Stueber, Gordy Knudtson, Dave DiCenso, Casey Scheuerell, Zoro, and Chris Coleman.

Active as a professional musician since 1998, Blake has performed across the United States with a wide variety of artists and bands at venues of all types including cafes, clubs, casinos, fairs, festivals, stadiums, and television. His drumming covers a wide range of contemporary music styles including rock, pop, R&B, funk, Latin, jazz, singer/songwriter, and country.

An active teacher and advocate for high quality music education, Blake has been teaching drum lessons since 2000. He currently teaches private lessons to students of all abilities in Los Angeles.

Blake is also the author of *Drumset Overlay: A Method for Developing Musical Drum Fills, Solos, and Grooves*.